The Rational Guide To:

SQL Server
Reporting Services

D1315325

PUBLISHED BY

Rational Press - An imprint of the Mann Publishing Group
208 Post Road, Suite 102
Greenland, NH 03840, USA
www.rationalpress.com
www.mannpublishing.com
+1 (603) 601-0325

ISBN: 0-9726888-9-7
Library of Congress Control Number (LCCN): 2004090129
Printed and bound in the United States of America.
10 9 8 7 6 5 4 3

Trademarks

Mann Publishing, Mann Publishing Group, Agility Press, Rational Press, Inc.Press, Farmhouse Press, The Rational Guide To, Rational Guides, ExecuGuide, AdminExpert, From the Source, the Mann Publishing Group logo, the Agility Press logo, the Rational Press logo, the Inc.Press logo, Timely Business Books, Rational Guides for a Fast-Paced World, and Custom Corporate Publications are all trademarks or registered trademarks of Mann Publishing Incorporated.

All brand names, product names, and technologies presented in this book are trademarks or registered trademarks of their respective holders.

Disclaimer of Warranty

While the publisher and author(s) have taken care to ensure accuracy of the contents of this book, they make no representation or warranties with respect to the accuracy or completeness of the contents of this book and specifically disclaim any implied warranties or merchantability or fitness for a specific purpose. The advice, strategies, or steps contained herein may not be suitable for your situation. You should consult with a professional where appropriate before utilizing the advice, strategies, or steps contained herein. Neither the publisher nor author(s) shall be liable for any loss of profit or any other commercial damages, including but not limited to special, incidental, consequential, or other damages.

Credits

Author:	Anthony T. Mann
Technical Editor:	Jason Carlson
Copy Editor:	Jeff Edman
Series Concept:	Anthony T. Mann
Cover Design:	Marcelo Paiva
Book Layout:	Marcelo Paiva

The Rational Guide To:

SQL Server
Reporting
Services

Anthony T. Mann

RATIONAL PRESS

An imprint of the

www.mannpublishing.com

About the Author

Anthony T. Mann is the President/CEO of the Mann Publishing Group, which specializes in publishing business and technology titles, including this book (under the Rational Press imprint). Holding the MCDBA, MCSD, and MCT certifications, he typically focuses on writing, teaching, publishing, and developing software with Microsoft-based technologies. His nine prior writings include *.NET Web Services for Dummies* (John Wiley & Sons), *Microsoft SQL Server 2000 for Dummies* (John Wiley & Sons), *SharePoint Portal Server: A Beginner's Guide* (Osborne/McGraw-Hill), and *Microsoft SQL Server 7 for Dummies* (John Wiley & Sons).

Acknowledgements

I would like to express my sincere appreciation to Marcelo Paiva, who has painstakingly produced this book and designed the cover. He has done an outstanding job under very difficult circumstances. I would also like to thank Jason Carlson for ensuring this book's technical accuracy and for providing great feedback and working so quickly. He accomplished these tasks while being swamped in getting SQL Server 2000 Reporting Services ready to ship at the end of January, 2004. I'd also like to thank Jeff Edman, whose superior editing skills were also instrumental in assuring this book's quality. Last, but certainly not least, I would like to thank my wife, Alison. Her unwavering support meant my countless late nights yielded a book of the highest quality.

Rational Guides for a
Fast-Paced World™

About Rational Guides

Rational Guides, from Rational Press, provide a no-nonsense approach to publishing based on both a practicality and price that make them rational. Rational Guides are compact books of fewer than 200 pages. Each Rational Guide is constructed with the highest quality writing and production materials—at a price of US$19.99 or less. All Rational Guides are intended to be as comprehensive as possible within the 200-page size constraint. Furthermore, all Rational Guides come with bonus materials, such as additional chapters, applications, code, utilities, or other resources. To download these materials, just register your book at www.rationalpress.com. See the instruction page at the end of this book to find out how to register your book.

Who Should Read This Book

Although this book is written for beginners, anyone who is new to Microsoft SQL Server Reporting Services should read it. This book not only explains the concepts surrounding SQL Server Reporting Services, but also shows step-by-step instructions on performing basic tasks that are typical in most organizations.

Conventions Used In This Book

The following conventions are used throughout this book:

► *Italics* — First introduction of a term.

► **Bold** — Exact name of an item or object that appears on the computer screen, such as menus, buttons, dropdown lists, or links.

► `Mono-spaced text` — Used to show a Web URL address, computer language code, or expressions as you must exactly type them.

Syntax for code, expressions, and formulas are show using this notation:

SYNTAX

```
http://<<server>>/<<ReportServer>>
```

EXAMPLE

```
http://reports.rationalpress.com/ReportServer
```

Tech Tip:
This box gives you additional technical advice about the option, procedure, or step being explained in the chapter.

Note:
This box gives you additional information to keep in mind as you read.

FREE *Bonus:*
This box lists additional free materials or content available on the Web after you register your book at www.rationalpress.com

Table of Contents

Table of Contents

Introduction

Chapter 1

An Overview of SQL Server Reporting Services

SQL Server Reporting Services is a set of innovative components and services that are part of Microsoft's overall Business Intelligence strategy. *Business Intelligence* is, quite simply, the ability to use technology to make better business decisions. These business decisions stem from an understanding of the vast amounts of data existing not only in large companies, but in small to medium-sized companies as well. In the past, many software vendors, including Microsoft, have targeted large companies for their Business Intelligence software. But that's about to change...

Prior approaches to Business Intelligence by leading vendors typically meant that only the largest companies could afford to implement these powerful solutions. For those companies that had the capital to invest in Business Intelligence, only select employees (typically analysts) were empowered to effectively sift through mountains of data to spot trends and patterns. Microsoft's new Business Intelligence strategy is to extend the technology in such a way that knowledge workers, analysts, middle managers, executives, and operations people alike can have access to the data they need to make better business decisions. This strategy is now being targeted at companies of all sizes. However, allowing all employees to use Business Intelligence tools doesn't mean that everyone can view sensitive data that doesn't pertain to them. The strategy is simply to empower users to have the tools they need to make better decisions. Issues relating to reporting security are covered in Chapter 9.

To set the stage, you should know a little about prior reporting solutions. In the past, reporting technologies had at least these problems:

► Reports were difficult to create.

► Reports were not accessible from other applications.

► Customization was limited.

► Long software development cycles made custom reports nearly impossible to attain - especially for small to medium-sized companies.

► Reports and corresponding data were usually not secure.

SQL Server Reporting Services is a comprehensive reporting platform whereby reports are stored on a centralized web server (or set of servers). Because reports are centralized, users run reports from one place. Having centralized reports also means that report deployment is quite simplified. In addition, because this platform sits on top of the Microsoft .NET Framework, the door is open to unlimited integration possibilities. In fact, all SQL Server Reporting Services is exposed as a set of Application Programming Interfaces (APIs) via Web Services. *Web Services* is an open mechanism that allows applications to integrate by using standard Internet technologies, such HTTP, SOAP, UDDI, and WSDL. Web Services are not just a set of Microsoft standards - they are industry standards.

SQL Server Reporting Services is made available as an add-on product to Microsoft SQL Server, beginning with SQL Server 2000. For more information on licensing and availability, visit the Microsoft web site at www.microsoft.com/sql.

So what's the big deal about SQL Server Reporting Services? Other reporting products have some cool features. Other reporting products run over the web. Some reporting products allow customization and yet others allow programming. All of this is true, but no other reporting solution offers such a comprehensive platform to achieve a best-of-breed solution. What's more is that SQL Server Reporting Services compiles reports into a .NET assembly. A *.NET assembly* is a unit of executable code that is managed by the Microsoft .NET framework to provide optimized services during the process of code execution. The .NET framework is a core component in all Microsoft technologies.

Let's See "The Goods!"

Before diving into what reporting services can do, it's important for you to see what a sample report looks like. Since SQL Server Reporting Services make reports centrally available on a web server, running a report from a PC can be done in a web browser such as Microsoft Internet Explorer. When you install SQL Server Reporting Services, a sample Visual Studio .NET project (called **SampleReports** by default) is also installed. Figure 1.1 shows what the sample report, called **Company Sales**, looks like at runtime in Internet Explorer.

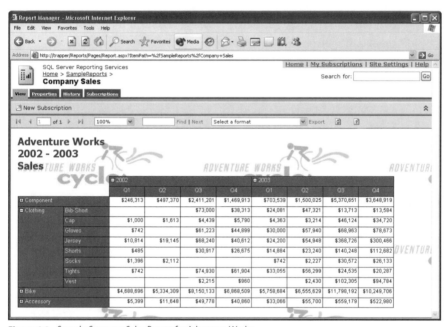

Figure 1.1 : Sample Company Sales Report for Adventure Works.

Figure 1.1 shows a sample report that is quite interactive. In other words, the sample **Company Sales** report allows you to drill up and down (by clicking the + and - links) to see more or less data detail. However, reports can be interactive in other ways as well. For example, you can search for specific data in the results, or even configure the report to supply filter criteria to limit data displayed on the report. An example of a filtered report would be one that displays sales only for the **Clothing** category. Adding interactivity to your reports is covered in Chapter 7.

Reporting Lifecycle

To provide true value, a SQL Server Reporting Services report is taken through an entire process, known as the reporting lifecycle. The *reporting lifecycle* is comprised of three separate activities:

- ► **Report Authoring** — The process of defining the report itself, report properties, user interactivity, and "look-and-feel." Report Authoring is covered in Part II of this book.

- ► **Report Management** — Activities centered on the administration of published report. Such activities include determining when reports are refreshed, who has access to those reports, and more. Report Management is covered in Part III of this book.

- ► **Report Delivery** — Activities focused on delivering reports to the end-users. You can specify the trigger for the delivery process (such as an event or user action) and the device on which the report shall be rendered (such as a PC browser, PDA, cell phone, or other mobile device). Report Delivery is covered in Part IV of this book.

Report Definition

The definition of each report is specified in XML and is stored in a file with an RDL file extension (which stands for Report Definition Language). RDL files can be generated using Visual Studio .NET 2003, or even your favorite text editor. After all, RDL files are simply XML, which is a text-based language. Therefore, any tool which can read or write XML will work fine. On the other hand, Visual Studio .NET 2003 has additional capabilities to allow you to design, debug, and test your reports from within a single integrated environment, so it's a good idea to use this tool to create and edit RDL files.

Defining a report generally includes these activities:

- ► Specifying one or more data sources that contain the data. SQL Server Reporting Services can access information from data sources, such as Microsoft SQL Server, OLE DB, ODBC, and Oracle. Data sources are covered in Chapter 4.

▶ Indicating which queries or stored procedures are used to retrieve data from a data source. The results of these queries are made available in a structure called a data set, which is also covered in Chapter 4.

▶ Placing graphical objects and elements on the report to show data, such as charts, graphs, and tables. There's even a special type of object, called a matrix. A *matrix* is a special object that is similar to a pivot table, which allows columns and rows to expand dynamically. Defining reports using these graphical elements is discussed in Chapter 5.

▶ Defining report options and criteria, such as parameters, sorting, grouping, and filtering. Customizing reports is shown in Chapter 6.

▶ Specifying security options, such as which users can access reports and what data they can see in those reports. Security of reports and data is covered in Chapter 9.

In Visual Studio .NET a single report is part of a larger project containing a set of reports that are developed together. Therefore, a reporting project likely contains multiple reports. One or more projects are contained within a solution. This follows the same concept as any other development project within Visual Studio .NET. To illustrate the file-to-project relationship, see Figure 1.2, which shows the same **Company Sales** report shown in Figure 1.1, but in the design-time environment of Visual Studio .NET 2003.

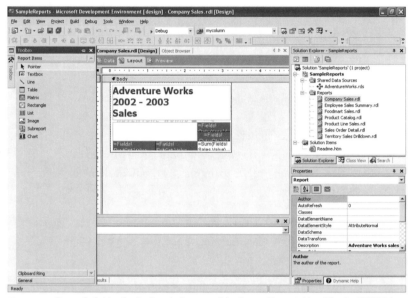

Figure 1.2: Report Definition for the Sample Company Sales Report Shown in Visual Studio .NET 2003.

You don't have to create all reports from scratch. If you have any reports stored in Microsoft Access 2002 (also known as Access XP), you can import those reports. However, because there is a difference in overall technology between SQL Server Reporting Services and Access 2002, you may not be able to import 100% of your Access reports. The good news is that you have an additional option to create reports by using the Report Wizard. The Report Wizard is discussed in Chapter 5.

Tech Tip:
You cannot import reports if your version of Microsoft Access is prior to version 2002.

Programmability

Since you know that reports are defined within Visual Studio .NET 2003, you won't be surprised to learn that virtually all aspects of a report or the reporting environment can be accessed programmatically. The bottom line is that you can make your reports behave exactly as your requirements dictate. The sky is the limit! All fields, report options, features, security settings, and more can be accessed and programmed using a rich set of objects available at runtime on the report server. You can even determine programmatically which server in a Web farm the report is running on. A *Web farm* is a series of servers that work together to spread incoming HTTP requests so that no single server reaches its processing limit. There are also statistics about the reports that you can access and analyze, such as how long your reports take to run, which reports are run most often, and so forth. Programmability of SQL Server Reporting Services is shown in Chapter 6.

Integration

Because of its native support for Web Services and related technologies, SQL Server Reporting Services supports tight integration with these commonly-used Microsoft products:

- ▶ Microsoft Internet Explorer

- ▶ Microsoft Office

- ▶ Microsoft SharePoint Portal Server

- ▶ Microsoft Windows SharePoint Services

SQL Server Reporting Services is powerful enough to develop reporting solutions that integrate with other popular Microsoft products right out of the box. Imagine a scenario where you create a reporting portal for use by your company to empower all knowledge workers to run reports from within the context of the portal or dashboard. For instance, you could configure a SharePoint Portal Server to show sales professionals new reports of their own personal sales every Monday morning. SharePoint Portal Server would cooperate with the reporting server to ensure that only the currently logged-in user could see the sensitive data. The possibilities are limitless! Integration with other products is discussed in Part IV of this book.

Deployment

Deployment with SQL Server Reporting Services is quite straightforward, since every .NET application is simple to deploy. Once the RDL files that comprise your reporting project(s) are written, they are compiled and deployed on the target reporting server. Deployment is covered in Chapter 11.

Security

The type of authentication supported by a requesting device dictates how the reporting server needs to handle security. Because every company handles security in different ways, multiple authentication schemes are available:

▶ **Basic Authentication** — Authenticates a user, but passwords are transmitted in clear text across a network. Credentials are not automatically encrypted.

▶ **NTLM** — Securely authenticates a user, following the encryption algorithm designed for Windows NT.

Tech Tip:
NTLM is formerly known as Challenge/Response authentication.

▶ **Passport** — Global centralized secure authentication scheme handled by Microsoft's Passport service.

▶ **Kerberos** — Secure authentication mechanism provided in Windows 2000 and later operating systems. Kerberos is harder to hack than NTLM and has support for strong passwords. This authentication method is recommended over NTLM when possible.

SQL Server Reporting Services follows a role-based security model. *Role-based security* is a model whereby a user login is associated with one or more roles (which usually mimic job functions). A role is associated with one or more privileges within the reporting system. Therefore, a single user login will likely have multiple privileges. For example, the system administrator role is allowed all privileges and can therefore perform all actions. On the other hand, a sales person might only have the privilege to view his/her own sales reports, but not a co-worker's sales reports. You can use the pre-installed security roles or create your own. Security and roles are covered further in Chapter 9. The following roles are automatically configured when you install SQL Server Reporting Services:

► **Browser** — Allows a user to view, but not change reports.

► **Content Manager** — Allows a user to manage the content of published reports.

► **My Reports** — Allows a user to manage all aspects of reports located in their personal **My Reports** folder.

► **Publisher** — Allows a user to publish reports to the report server.

Delivery

Delivery refers to the ability of SQL Server Reporting Services to render a report in a particular format and send it to the target location. Reports can be generated in any of the following formats:

► **HTML** (for web pages and other HTML compatible programs, both HTML 3.2 and 4.0)

► **HTML with the Office Web Components**

► **Web Archive file**

► **CSV** (comma separated values, or any delimiter)

► **TIFF File** (as a printable snapshot image, or any other image format: BMP, JPG, PNG, WMF)

► **Excel Document** (if using Office XP or later)

► **XML** (eXtensible Markup Language)

► **PDF File** (for using Adobe Acrobat)

In addition to the output format of the reports, you can also indicate the timing and location of the report delivery in a subscription. In other words, subscriptions can be generated under the following conditions:

► **On Demand** — Reports are rendered when the user requests a report to be run. Large reports might take considerable time to run, so you have the option of configuring reports to use a cached (or snapshot) copy of the report. Using cached data speeds up report querying because the report does not have to process data every time a user requests the report.

► **Simple Subscription** — Reports are generated upon certain events (such as data changing) or time schedules (such as every Sunday night) and pushed to a client device or computer from the reporting server.

► **Data-driven Subscription** — Reports are generated automatically, just as in a simple subscription, but also allows a query to be written and applied to the delivery of a report at runtime. This allows you to create subscriptions to reports based on parameters or recipients that are not known at the time the subscription is created.

Reports can be delivered to a list of recipients via e-mail or placed on a network file share. Additional delivery options can be customized by writing your own delivery extensions. Subscriptions are covered in Chapter 12.

Editions

SQL Server Reporting Services is available from Microsoft in these editions:

▶ **Standard** — Includes basic features, such as:

- Report rendering and delivery

- Simple (push) subscriptions

- Role-based security

- Exporting to multiple file formats

- Support for up to 2GB RAM

- Support for up to 4 processors

▶ **Enterprise** — Includes all Standard Edition features, plus:

- Data-driven subscriptions

- Web farm support

- Custom authentication

- Support for more than 2GB RAM

- Support for more than 4 processors

▶ **Developer** — Same as the Enterprise Edition, but will also install on Windows XP. The Developer Edition cannot be deployed onto a production server.

▶ **Evaluation** — Same as the Enterprise Edition, but will expire after the trial period ends.

What Can SQL Server Reporting Services Do?

Starting with SQL Server 2000, SQL Server Reporting Services extends Microsoft's Business Intelligence platform to allow control over most aspects of your reports, such as:

► Report Definition

► Programmability

► Integration

► Deployment

► Security

► Delivery

Summary

SQL Server Reporting Services is a revolutionary new technology that allows you to gain complete control over all your reporting needs. You can feel confident that all of your data is stored securely and will be safe from unauthorized users. Finally, reports can be rendered in a variety of popular formats and displayed on PCs, PDAs, cell phones, and other mobile devices.

The rest of this book explores these topics in greater depth. You'll learn how to create, manage, deploy, and use reports created with SQL Server Reporting Services. If you're ready to dive in, let's begin…

Chapter 2

SQL Server Reporting Services Architecture

Before you dive into using SQL Server Reporting Services, it can be quite helpful to have a basic understanding of the SQL Server Reporting Services architecture. The *architecture* refers to the internal components of the report server, which is at the core of SQL Server Reporting Services. The architecture also refers to the basic external functional blocks that interact with the report server. This chapter outlines these concepts and also the hardware and software requirements for installing the server.

Report Server Architecture

The report server is comprised of a set of services that handle all aspects of processing, rendering, scheduling, and delivering reports. Furthermore, the report server facilitates the management of your reports and configuration by making available a web-based application called Report Manager. *Report Manager* is an application written in Visual C# (one of the languages supported by Visual Studio .NET) that uses the interfaces exposed by the report server. Figure 2.1 shows how these pieces fit together in the overall architecture of SQL Server Reporting Services.

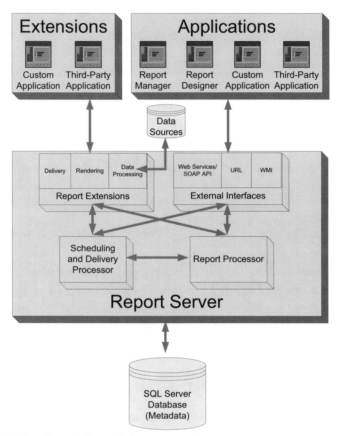

Figure 2.1: SQL Server Reporting Services Architecture.

Report Server

The report server itself consists mainly of a report processor and a scheduling and delivery processor. The report processor is responsible for controlling all aspects of reporting, such as getting metadata out of the database, communicating with the data sources, and sending data to the rendering extensions, so that data can be rendered in the desired format. The scheduling and delivery processor simply handles the scheduling of running reports and also delivers them to the target user. For example, if a subscription is configured to deliver a report every week to a user via e-mail, the scheduling and delivery processor is responsible for doing this.

There are two services used by SQL Server Reporting Services – a Web Service and an NT (Windows) service. The NT service handles all background tasks such as scheduling and delivery. The NT service does not have an exposed interface or API for you to access. Its purpose is to read from the metadata database. Report processing is hosted by both of these services. The Web Service handles all live requests from your programs and Report Manager. Report processing does not communicate with anything other than the service that is hosting it and the data source via the data source extension.

Applications

SQL Server Reporting Services exposes three types of external interfaces that applications can use to interact with the report server. This includes third-party applications as well as your own applications. The external interfaces supported are:

► **Web Services** — An industry standard integration interface that uses Internet technologies, such as HTML, HTTP, WSDL, and XML.

► **URL** (Uniform Resource Locator) — An Internet address using the HTTP or HTTPS protocol that includes parameters to instruct the report server how to render the report, what arguments to use, and more.

► **WMI** (Windows Management Instrumentation) — A specification and interface for controlling the management of your reporting server.

The Report Manager application itself uses the Web Services interface to allow users to manage security, data sources, reports, and parameters. Report Manager will also run reports and schedule subscriptions. If you wish, you can use the Web Services interface and any supported .NET language to create an application that performs the same functionality as Report Manager. Supported languages include Visual Basic .NET, Visual C++ .NET, Visual C# .NET, and Visual J# .NET. If you don't want to use Visual Studio .NET, you can use the exposed SOAP API. The SOAP API can be accessed from any language on any platform.

Extensions

SQL Server Reporting Services is completely extensible. Although these advanced topics are not covered in this book, you should know that you can write your own programs to extend the functionality of SQL Server Reporting Services. You can extend these functional areas:

▶ **Delivery** — Allows you to write custom extensions that offer additional functionality over the standard E-Mail and File Share delivery extensions.

▶ **Rendering** — Allows you to write custom extensions to render into formats that are not supported out of the box. Example formats that you could write would be ZIP archives and RTF files.

▶ **Data Processing** — Allows you to write custom extensions to grab data from additional data sources. For example, you can write a custom extension to retrieve data from SAP, JD Edwards, or Siebel.

Refer to the SQL Server Reporting Services online help for more information about custom extensions.

Hardware Requirements

Microsoft recommends installing SQL Server Reporting Services on hardware that meets the minimum requirements outlined in Table 2.1.

COMPONENT	REQUIREMENT
Processor	Intel Pentium II, 500MHZ
Memory	256MB
Disk Space (Without Samples)	80MB
Disk Space (With Samples)	225MB

Table 2.1: Minimum Report Server Hardware Requirements.

The hardware requirements shown in Table 2.1 should be used as an absolute minimum. The more hardware resources you can allocate, the better the server will run. The price of hardware has dropped dramatically over the years, so getting a high-powered server is a very inexpensive way to achieve higher performance.

Software Requirements

Table 2.2 lists the minimum software requirements necessary for the report server itself. There are separate software requirements if you are going to develop reports for use on the reporting server, which are covered in the section "Developer Workstation," later in this chapter.

COMPONENT	REQUIREMENT
Web Server	Internet Information Services (IIS), version 5.0 with ASP.NET configured
.NET Framework	Version 1.1
Data Access Components	MDAC 2.6
Operating System	Windows 2000 (Server, Advanced Server, or Datacenter editions*) with Service Pack 4 or Windows 2003 Server (Standard, Enterprise, or Datacenter editions*) * Depending on the SQL Server Reporting Services edition you are using.
Disk Space (With Samples)	225MB

Table 2.2: Minimum Report Server Software Requirements.

Database

The report server uses two SQL Server databases in its everyday operations. These databases are automatically created when you installed SQL Server Reporting Services.

The first database, named **ReportServer** by default, is used to store configuration data known as metadata. *Metadata* is used by SQL Server Reporting Services to configure important configurations like data sources, users, policies, roles, and so forth.

The second database, named **ReportServerTempDB** by default, is used to store temporary information, such as session data and working snapshot data. Everything in the **ReportServerTempDB** database is fluid and is automatically recreated when necessary.

For hardware and software requirements for the SQL Server database, refer to the SQL Server online help or the Microsoft web site. The only requirement imposed by SQL Server Reporting Services on the database server is that it must have Service Pack 3 or later installed.

Developer Workstation

The development of reports is typically done on a developer workstation. The reports are developed using a tool that can write XML files, such as Visual Studio .NET 2003. There are no specific hardware requirements for the developer workstation. Table 2.3 shows the software requirements needed to develop reports and to install the client components necessary to facilitate deployment of reports on the report server.

COMPONENT	REQUIREMENT
Web Server	Internet Information Services (IIS), version 5.0 with ASP.NET configured
.NET Framework	Version 1.1
Data Access Components	MDAC 2.6
Operating System	Windows 2000 – Any edition, with Service Pack 4 installed or Windows XP with Service Pack 1 installed
Development Tool	Visual Studio .NET 2003

Table 2.3: Minimum Developer Workstation Software Requirements.

Summary

An overall understanding of the architecture, hardware, and software requirements can be quite helpful before diving into creating reports and using SQL Server Reporting Services. It is very important to understand that the Report Manager application was built using the same external interfaces that are available to your own applications. It is important because you can feel confident that the external interfaces provide enough functionality for your own applications to be extensible. In addition, you can write custom delivery, rendering, and data processing extensions to extend the functionality of SQL Server Reporting Services. The bottom line is that complete flexibility and extensibility were designed to be part of the product.

Chapter 3

Designing Effective Reports

Before you dive into creating your reports with SQL Server Reporting Services, you must plan your report. After all, how can you create a report if you don't know what you're creating? A common problem is that a developer thinks he/she knows how to develop the report, but doesn't actually have any requirements, so invariably the final report doesn't meet the user's needs.

To design effective and usable reports, at a minimum, you should consider:

- ► What are the requirements from users?

- ► How will data be presented on the report?

- ► What type of interactivity will be used on the report?

- ► Will the user be able to filter data?

- ► What level of security is needed for the report?

- ► How will you manage the development lifecycle?

This short chapter deals with these issues. It is designed to help you think about the criteria for designing effective reports. It is a good idea to consider the points made in this chapter as you read through the rest of this book.

User Requirements

User requirements are a very important part of the process of designing effective reports. If you create a report without user requirements, you will find yourself in a situation where you are never finished designing and creating the report. The amount of detailed user input you receive will vary according to the processes imposed by your organization. Some organizations do not elicit detailed specifications from their users, so it is up to the IT department to determine what the user's requirements are. Do not underestimate the importance of clearly-defined requirements as a means of knowing the needs of users.

Data Presentation

Users don't care how easy or difficult it is to do any programming or custom software development. All they know is what they see. That's why data presentation is so important. It is important to test the data presentation in a report against user requirements, but data presentation is also important for aesthetic reasons. Users like attractive screens, with graphics, logos, charts, and more. However, you can go overboard with these items - especially if they aren't adding any value to the report itself.

Headers and Footers

Headers and footers are very important elements of a report. A *header* is printed at the top of every data page in a report, while a *footer* is printed at the bottom. You don't necessarily need both, but you should consider that a single page from a printed report might very easily become separated from the other pages in the report. The reader of the single page should have a context for the following:

► Which report the page came from

► The date (and perhaps time) the report was generated

► The page number from the report

These points can all be addressed using headers, footers, or a combination of both.

Grouping

Grouping refers to what happens when there is a change in value of the field(s) that make up a group. This is very similar to how SQL queries can contain the **GROUP BY** clause to calculate aggregates based on grouped data. However, report grouping is not only related to data, but to how the report physically looks when there is a change of the grouping value. For example, you can have the report generate a page break upon the change in value of the sales division field.

Interactivity

SQL Server Reporting Services is one of the few tools on the market that allows you to build significant interactivity into your reports. Adding interactivity to your reports is discussed in Chapter 7. Your reports can include:

▶ Parameters that must be specified by the user

▶ Drilldown reports that allow a user to choose the level of detail required with the few clicks of the mouse

▶ Drillthrough reports that allow you to run one report from another report

▶ Document maps that allow very fast navigation to a specific page in the report

▶ Jumping to a specific page in the report

▶ Searching for specific data within the report

▶ Exporting data into a wide variety of formats

▶ Zooming to any level of detail

Filtering Data

Filtering data refers to the limitation of the data that is displayed on your report. It is very important to filter your data for two main reasons:

1   Without filtering data, potentially all rows in one or more tables can be retrieved into your report. This can lead to very poor performance of your report generation and overall server degradation.

2   Users can select exactly the data that pertains to them. For example, if a user only cares about data for Q1 of 2004, you should allow them to filter the data based on parameters whose values are specified at runtime.

Filtering data can be accomplished by designing parameters into your report, specifying **WHERE** clause information in your data sets, or both. Parameters are discussed in Chapter 7, while data sets are shown in Chapter 4.

Security

Security of data is one of the most important things to consider when designing your reports. Security is discussed in detail in Chapter 9. SQL Server Reporting Services allows you to configure and specify security in these areas:

▶   Data sources

▶   SSL encryption

▶   Report execution and rendering

▶   Listing and viewing available reports

▶   Folders

▶   Server settings

Make sure that you consider security to be of utmost importance and never stop thinking about security as you continue to design your reports. You don't want to have to learn that someone's data, such as salary information, is now a matter of public record because you didn't secure your reports.

Performance

Every action that you perform when designing and implementing your reports should always consider how performance will be impacted. This is true for everything from designing your reports to constructing your queries. Remember, even if your decision seems to have a minimal effect on performance, it will be multiplied many times as you design the rest of your reports and have many users run those reports. The bottom line is that every little bit counts!

The Development Lifecycle

Effectively designing a report itself is only one part of the equation. The other part is how you will test and deploy those reports. If you don't have a process in place to manage the development lifecycle, you risk deploying the wrong version of a report or a reporting project. If you don't have a testing environment in place, you risk having problems with one or more reports when many users access the report simultaneously. If your budget allows, it is a good idea to use an automated testing tool that will simulate a large load on the server. This will help determine if your report will "break" when multiple users access it simultaneously. You might find, for example, that the queries that make up your data sets are actually blocking each other. This is something you would not easily find if you were the only one testing your reports or if you did not test your reports under load.

It is also a good idea to implement some form of source code versioning or control, such as Microsoft SourceSafe. Source code control is vital in keeping tight reigns over specific builds of your source code. It also allows you to revert to an older version if necessary. Source code control software follows a check-in/check-out paradigm to avoid multiple people from making changes to the same code at the same time.

Summary

There is no single way to design effective reports, but there are many guidelines that you can consider as you learn how SQL Server Reporting Services works throughout the rest of this book. Keep the elements discussed in this short chapter in mind. Even though they are simple points, they are very important. Your users will appreciate it.

Authoring
Reports

Chapter 4

Data Sources
and Data Sets

Before you can create a report with SQL Server 2000 Reporting Services, you must specify from which source of data the report will be created, known as a *data source*. After you specify where the report will get its data, you indicate the query that will retrieve data from that data source, known as a *data set*. This chapter shows you how to specify the data sources and data sets to be used in your report.

Data Sources

A data source is just that...a source of data. A data source is the name given to a collection of properties that describe and specify how your reports connect to data. These properties, specified in a *connection string*, differ depending on the type of data source, but generally include logon information, names of databases, security parameters, and more. A reporting services data source can be any of the following:

- ▶ **SQL Server** — Connects to any SQL Server (version 7 or later) using the SQL Server data provider that is built into the Microsoft .NET framework.

- ▶ **Oracle** — Connects to an Oracle database using the Oracle Call Interface (OCI) data provider that is built into the Microsoft .NET framework.

▶ **ODBC** (**O**pen **D**ata **B**ase Connectivity) — A very standard, backward-compatible data source type that can be used for any vendor that allows ODBC connectivity to their data source.

▶ **OLE DB** (**O**bject **L**inking and **E**mbedding for **D**ata **B**ases) — A Microsoft-based technology that is faster than ODBC, and allows other advanced connections, such as SQL Server Analysis Services.

▶ **Custom** — Allows any non-standard technology to be used as a data source, but requires custom data extensions to be developed for SQL Server Reporting Services.

Regardless of the type of data source that your reports will use, each uses a connection string to specify the properties of the data source type and supplies information for locating and connecting to the data source.

Data Source Scopes

There are two scopes available to your data sources. A *scope* determines the visibility of a data source. These data source scopes are available to your data sources:

▶ **Shared** — Allows you to define a data source and use it among many different reports. In a shared data source, the definition that makes up the data source is stored in a common location on the report server. Shared data sources are very useful when many reports use identical connection information.

▶ **Report** — Allows you to specify a data source for each report individually. A report data source is actually stored within the definition of the report itself, not in a common location, as in the case of a shared data source.

Managing Shared Data Sources

There are two ways to manage (create, edit, and delete) data sources. You can use either the report server administrative web page, called Report Manager, or a Visual Studio .NET 2003 project. Each is outlined in the following sections.

Report Manager

To access Report Manager to manage your data sources, follow these simple steps:

1   Enter the Report Manager URL into your browser, using this syntax:

SYNTAX

http://<<server>>/<<ReportsFolder>>

EXAMPLE

http://www.rationalpress.com/Reports

2   Click the **New Data Source** button. This brings up the screen shown in Figure 4.1 to allow you to configure your new data source.

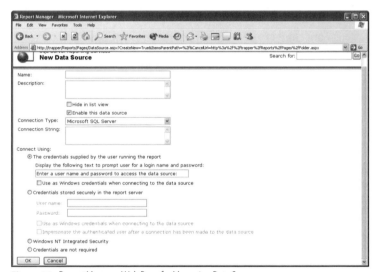

Figure 4.1: Report Manager Web Page for Managing Data Sources.

3   Configuring a data source is as simple as filling in the properties on the screen, as follows:

- **Name** — The name of your data source. This is the name that you will use within your reports, so don't make it too cryptic. This field is mandatory.

- **Description** — A description of what this data source will be used for. This field is optional.

- **Hide in list view** — If checked, this option will prevent the data source from appearing on the Report Manager web page. This option is unchecked by default.

- **Enable this data source** — If checked, this option will allow you to use this data source. This option is checked by default.

- **Connection Type** — Choose the type of connection for the data source.

- **Connection String** — This string is used to tell the data source definition how to connect to the data source. The parameters of the connection string will depend on the type of connection selected. The connection string for a SQL Server data source looks like this, but can vary according to additional options that you specify:

SYNTAX

```
Data source=<<server>>;initial catalog=<<database>>
```

EXAMPLE

```
Data source=sql4.rationalpress.com;initial catalog=ReportDB
```

- **Connect Using** — Specify how you would like to connect to your data source. You have these options for specifying security:

  - **The credentials supplied by the user running the report** — Prompts the user for the user name and password as the report is run. If you select this option, you can further supply the text to prompt the user. If the credentials supplied are Windows credentials rather than data source credentials, this option must be selected so that the Report Server can impersonate the Windows user before connecting to the data source.

- **Credentials stored securely in the report server** —
  Stores the supplied credentials in an encrypted format on
  the reporting server. If you choose this option, you also
  enter a **User name** and **Password** to store on the reporting
  server.

- **Windows NT Integrated Security** — This option will
  use the credentials of the currently logged-in user. This is
  known as single sign-on (or SSO).

- **Credentials are not required** — This option will not use
  any credentials when connecting to the data source. It is
  not recommended to use this option, as this is the least
  secure choice for connecting to a data source.

> *Note:*
> The Credentials are not required option only works if you specify
> the unattended user account using the RSConfig Tool after setup.

4   Click the **OK** button to create a data source based on the criteria
    you have selected.

If you wish to edit, delete, or move the data source, you can do this:

1   Navigate to the desired folder containing the data source in Report
    Manager.

2   Ensure that you have clicked the **Show Details** button. If this button
    is already clicked, you will see a **Hide Details** button, as this is a
    toggle feature.

3   To edit your data source, click the icon in the **Edit** column and
    change the desired fields.

4   To delete your data source, click the check box in the left-hand
      column associated with your data source, followed by the **Delete**
      button.

5   To move your data source, click the check box in the left-hand
      column associated with your data source, and then click the **Move**
      button. You will be prompted to select a target folder for the
      selected data source.

Visual Studio .NET 2003 Project

Another way to specify a data source is to do so in your Reporting Services project
within Visual Studio .NET 2003. The Visual Studio .NET 2003 environment
(also known as the *IDE*, or Integrated Development Environment) is covered in
more depth in Chapter 5. To configure a data source within the IDE, follow these
instructions:

1   Open Visual Studio .NET 2003.

2   Right-click the **Shared Data Sources** folder.

3   Click the **Add New Data Source** menu. Clicking this menu brings
      up the **Data Link Properties** dialog box shown in Figure 4.2.

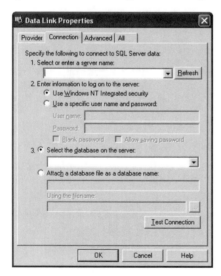

Figure 4.2: Configuring Data Link Properties.

4   Configure the data link properties in the dialog box. By default, a new data source will connect to a SQL Server database. If you wish to change this, choose the desired provider in the **Provider** tab. Otherwise, fill in these fields:

  • **Select or enter a server name** — The name of the server to connect to. This field is mandatory.

  • **Enter information to log on to the server** — Select the **Use Windows NT Integrated security** option if your SQL server uses **Windows only** authentication. Otherwise, if your server uses **SQL Server and Windows** authentication, select the **Use a specific user name and password** option and enter the logon information in the **User name** and **Password** text boxes. This field is mandatory.

  • **Select the database on the server** — Select the desired database from the dropdown list. This field is mandatory.

5   Click the **Test** button to verify your configuration parameters and test the security for the connection.

Managing Report Data Sources

If you don't want your data source to be stored in a central place on the server for use by multiple reports, you can embed the data source information inside the definition of the report. If you do this, you cannot use the web-based Report Manager. To create report-specific data sources, you must use a Visual Studio .NET 2003 report project or edit the Report Definition Language (RDL) file using another text editor.

To manage report-specific data sources, follow these steps:

1   Open Visual Studio .NET 2003.

2   Create a new report or open an existing report. Creating reports is covered in Chapter 5.

3   Click the **Data** tab. By default, the Generic Query Designer is
    shown. Use the Generic Query Designer to specify the text of the
    query if you know it. Otherwise, use the Visual Query Designer.
    The Visual Query Designer can be shown by deselecting the
    Generic Query Designer button. The Generic/Visual Query
    Designer button is shown in Figure 4.3.

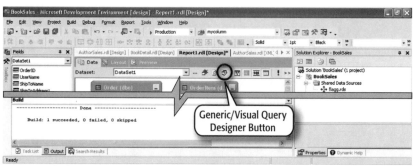

Figure 4.3: Configuring a Data Set with the Visual Query Designer.

4   Click the Ellipsis button (**…**) next to the **Dataset** dropdown list,
    which brings up the dialog box shown in Figure 4.4.

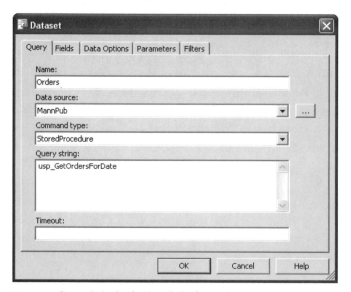

Figure 4.4: Dataset Dialog Box for Manually Configuring Properties.

5   Click the Ellipsis button (**...**) next to the **Data source** dropdown
     list, which brings up the dialog box shown in Figure 4.5.

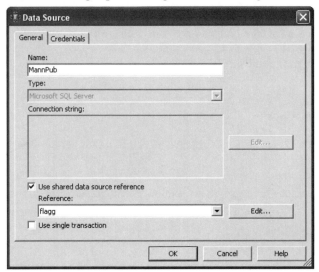

Figure 4.5: Data Source Dialog Box.

6   Uncheck the **Use shared data source reference** option to enable
     the **Connection string** text box.

7   Enter the connection string information associated with your
     database connection.

8   Click the **Credentials** tab and enter the security information
     associated with your new data source.

9   Click the **OK** button to save your changes and close the dialog box.

Data Sets

A data set is the result of a query against a data source. If you are using SQL,
specify the columns of data that will be used as the basis of data for your report,
along with joins between tables and any restrictions in the number of rows that
are returned. Data sets can come from tables, views, or stored procedures. You
can create a data set from within the Visual Studio .NET 2003 environment
in a report project. Your data sets can specify queries from tables or stored

procedures. Each type of data set query is outlined in the next two sections.

Data Sets from Tables or Views

To configure a data set using tables or views, follow these steps:

1   Open Visual Studio .NET 2003.

2   Create a new report or open an existing report. Creating reports is covered in Chapter 5.

3   Click the **Data** tab. Clicking this tab brings up the screen shown in Figure 4.3.

4   Deselect the Generic Query Designer button to show the Visual Query Designer. The rest of this procedure assumes you are using the Visual Query Designer.

5   Add the tables that will participate in the query by right-clicking anywhere in the table area and clicking the **Add table** menu. Alternatively, you can add views and functions as well, by clicking the applicable tab.

6   Select the desired tables for the query.

7   Default join information (shown with a connecting line between tables) is automatically known if your database was defined with referential integrity, via foreign keys. If you need to alter the joins between tables, drag and drop from one field in a table to another to create a join in your query.

8   Click the check boxes next to the columns in the tables that will be returned from the query. These are the columns that the report will be able to use.

9   Enter filter criteria if you want to limit the number of records returned. Do this by entering the desired filter value in the **Criteria** column associated with the column returned from the query.

10   Test the query by clicking the **Run** button.

The data set configuration will be saved along with the report.

Data Sets from Stored Procedures

To configure a data set to use a stored procedure, follow the same procedure as you do for tables (see the section "Data Sets from Tables or Views," earlier in this chapter), but instead of adding tables to your data set, click the ellipsis button (**...**), which brings up the dialog box shown in Figure 4.4.

Follow these steps to configure your data set to use a stored procedure:

1   Select **StoredProcedure** from the **Command type** dropdown list.

2   In the **Query string** text box, enter the name of your stored procedure exactly as it is defined in your database.

3   Click the **Fields** tab. You'll see a list of the fields that are returned from the stored procedure. If necessary, click the **X** button to remove fields from your dataset.

4   Click the **Parameters** tab to configure how the parameters of a stored procedure get their values.

5   Click the **Filters** tab to limit the number of rows that are returned as part of the data set. Filters are covered in Chapter 7.

6   Click the **OK** button to save your changes and close the dialog box.

Summary

Reports in SQL Server Reporting Services get their data from data sources and data sets. There are many options when creating data sources and data sets. Data sources can be stored on the report server itself as a shared data source for all reports to use. Alternatively, data source definitions can be stored within the report itself. Storing the data source in the report definition makes the report more portable, but less secure. Data sets are created by querying the data source and, if using SQL, specifying the tables or stored procedure containing the source data. This chapter outlined all of these options and guided you through the process of creating data sources and data sets.

Chapter 5

The Report
Design Environment

The *Report Design Environment* is where you create and manage the source of your reports. It is called an environment because it actually consists of an entire suite of tools that work together to boost productivity and enhance the total development experience. The Report Design Environment is sometimes referred to as the Integrated Development Environment, or *IDE*.

The IDE used to create reports for SQL Server Reporting Services is Visual Studio .NET, version 2003 or later. When you installed the client components for SQL Server Reporting Services, special add-ins to the IDE were also installed so that you can create reporting projects. There are two types of reporting services projects that you can create from within the Visual Studio .NET 2003 IDE:

▶ **Report Project Wizard** — Creates a new Visual Studio .NET
2003 project inside a solution and guides you through the process of
creating a report, using some basic options and prompts. This is the
easiest way to create reports.

▶ **Report Project** — Creates a new Visual Studio .NET 2003 project
inside a solution and does not create any reports within the project.
You must create your reports at a later time.

This chapter guides you through the process of learning how to use the IDE to create report projects and reports within those projects, either manually or by using the wizard. This chapter also shows you the new tools in your toolbox that can be used to create and enhance your reports.

Note:

This chapter assumes that you already know the basic concepts of how to use the Visual Studio .NET environment. This chapter points out only the Reporting Services-specific features within the environment.

Creating Projects

Before you can create any reports, you must create a Visual Studio .NET project. This project acts as the container for your reports, data sources, images, and all other report-related files.

To create a new project, follow these steps:

1   Start Visual Studio .NET 2003.

2   Click the **New Project** button.

3   In the **New Project** dialog box, shown in Figure 5.1, click the **Business Intelligence Projects** folder. You will see the types of projects that you can create, called *templates*.

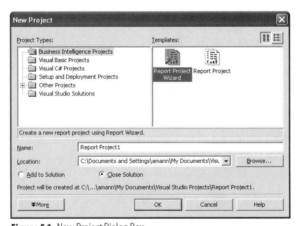

Figure 5.1: New Project Dialog Box.

4   Click the type of project desired from the available templates, give the project a **Name** and **Location**, then click the **OK** button. If you choose the **Report Project Wizard** template, your project will be created and the Report Wizard will be automatically invoked. To see how to use this wizard, refer to the section, "Using the Report Wizard," later in this chapter. If you choose the **Report Project** template, the wizard takes no further action.

Creating New Reports

Once you have created a Visual Studio .NET report project, the next task is to create one or more reports within that project. There are two ways of creating a report.

The first way of creating a report is to use the Report Wizard, which guides you through the process of creating a report and configuring its data sources. The second way of creating a report is to configure an empty report shell without placing any graphical or data elements. The latter is useful if you want to maintain complete control over your reports, but requires more effort because nothing is configured automatically.

Using the Report Wizard

If the Report Wizard is not automatically invoked (because you didn't create a project by using the **Report Project Wizard** template), you can launch the wizard at any time within your Visual Studio .NET project by right-clicking the **Reports** folder in the Solution Explorer pane and clicking the **Add New Report** menu.

The Report Wizard guides you through these steps:

1   At the **Welcome** screen, click the **Next** button.

2   The **Select the Data Source** step is the first step you see. This step is used to indicate where the report should get its data. You can create a new data source, or select an existing shared data source. Data sources are covered in Chapter 4. Click the **Next** button to move to step 3.

3   In the **Design the Query** screen, enter the query string that will be used to select data from your data source. This query string, known as a *data set*, is any valid statement for the data source being used. For example, the query string would be in a SQL format for Microsoft SQL Server. You can enter the statement in the text box provided, or use the query builder by clicking the Ellipsis button (**...**). More information about using the query builder and data sets can be found in Chapter 4. Click the **Next** button to go to step 4.

4   In the **Select the Report Type** screen, you must define the type of report the wizard is to create. You can choose **Tabular** or **Matrix**. A *tabular* report is used to show a report that typically lists data where a cross-tab display is not necessary. An example of a tabular report is a screen that displays the entire contents from the query of a table. The region of the screen that shows a tabular report is known as a *table*. A *matrix* report is called a cross-tab report. An example of a cross-tab report would be a screen that shows royalties by author, where months might be displayed across the top, and authors down the left-hand side. Click the **Next** button to proceed to step 5.

5   In this step, you will design your table or matrix, depending on the option chosen in step 4. This step allows you to specify which fields from the data set specified in step 3 will be used on the report. You have these choices:

   •   **Page** — Any fields that you add to this section will be displayed on the top of every report and a page break will occur when the value of this field changes during the rendering of this report. For example, you might do a page break for every author in an author sales report. This option is available for tabular and matrix reports.

- **Group** — Fields added to this section will cause the report to break when this value changes. For example, you might want a new group for every change in distribution channel for book sales. This option is available only for tabular reports.

- **Details** — Details are line-item values at the most granular level. For example, details might be the actual sales figures for each book's author, based on month and sales channel. This option is available for tabular and matrix reports.

- **Columns** — This box specifies the fields whose values will be grouped and displayed across the top part of the report. For example, you may have a report that will display the month in a given year for all sales as a column. This option is available only for matrix reports.

- **Rows** — This box specifies the fields whose values will be grouped and displayed in the left-hand column of a report. An example of a row is the sales channel for all sales in a given year. This option is available only for matrix reports.

- **Enable drilldown** — This check box specifies that a user can *drilldown*, or display more detailed data at a further level of granularity. By default, only the least granular grouping will be visible when viewing the report. For a matrix report, both rows and columns will be collapsed. Drilldown is discussed in Chapter 7. This option is available only for matrix reports.

To place a field in the desired area, simply click the field in the **Available fields** listbox. Click the corresponding button to add the selected field to the appropriate section. When you are finished adding fields, click the **Next** button to move to the next step.

6   This step is only available if you chose the **Tabular** report type in step 4. In this step, shown in the **Choose the Table Layout** screen, you will indicate how the tabular data is to be displayed. You have these choices:

- **Stepped** — Displays group headers in a "stepped" fashion, showing group headers to the left of each detail field rather than directly above it, as in the case of a **Block** report.

- **Block** — Displays group header rows for every change in the grouped values for each detail column. Contrary to a **Stepped** report, a **Block** report displays headers directly above each detail field.

- **Include subtotals** — Forces the report to automatically include subtotal fields for numeric fields in each grouping. Due to the way reports are physically laid out on the page, checking this field yields different placement of the subtotal fields, depending on whether you selected **Stepped** or **Block**. For **Stepped** reports, subtotals are placed in the group header, allowing for drilldown capability. For **Block** reports, subtotals are placed in the group footer.

- **Enable drilldown** — Checking this option allows you to drilldown into the details of your report. If you select this option, the report will not show the details - only the totals. The report will display a **+** sign, indicating that you can manually drilldown into the details.

Click the **Next** button to continue.

7   This step allows you to specify the style of your report. The wizard screen gives you a great preview as to the "look-and-feel" of the style. You have these choices:

- **Bold** — Gives your reports a strong impact using a bold typeface and dark colors.

- **Casual** — Gives your reports a colorful look without being very bold.

- **Compact** — Uses less space when there are many columns of data on your report.

- **Corporate** — Uses the typical blue and gray colors found in many conservative businesses.

- **Plain** — Does not format the report with any style.

After you choose a style, click **Next.**

8   In the **Choose the Deployment Location** step, you indicate the deployment target for your report. This step only appears if the project is a new one, which means that the deployment target has never been set for the project. Simply fill in these fields:

- **Report Server** — Specifies the URL of the report server. The format for the URL is:

  SYNTAX
  ```
  http://<<server>>/<<ReportServer>>
  ```

  EXAMPLE
  ```
  http://reports.rationalpress.com/ReportServer
  ```

- **Deployment folder** — Indicates which folder on the report server will receive the deployed reports as part of your project. For our example, we will deploy to a folder named **BookSales**. Click **Next** to jump to the last step.

9   The **Completing the Report Wizard** step allows you to do a few things. First, specify the name of your report. This is the name that will appear to your users, so choose a name that fits the way you will use the report.

The second thing this step allows is a review of all the options you have chosen in prior steps. If you have any changes to make, click the **Back** button and correct any problems.

The last task in this step is to preview the report after it is created by clicking the **Preview report** check box. Click the **Finish** button to create your report.

You can display your reports in one of three separate views, as illustrated in Figure 5.2. Views are represented as a series of tabs:

▶ **Data** — The *data view* allows you to select the data sources and data sets that will be used on your reports. The example in Figure 5.2 shows the data view using a stored procedure as the data source. The data view is displayed by default after you create an empty report.

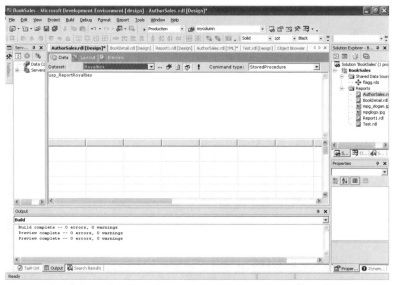

Figure 5.2: Sample Design-Time Matrix Report in Data View, Showing a Stored Procedure as a Data Set.

▶ **Layout** — The *layout view* allows you to place fields on the report, control the "look-and-feel" of the report, and specify property values for the report. The layout view is shown by default after you create a report with the Report Wizard. Figure 5.3 shows the layout view.

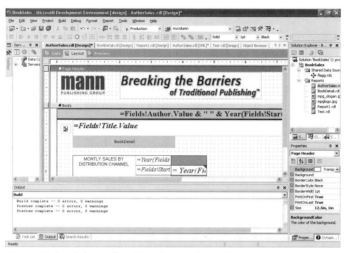

Figure 5.3: Sample Design-Time Matrix Report in Layout View.

▶ **Preview** — The *preview view* shows you what the report will look like by rendering it on your workstation. You can preview your report before you deploy it onto your testing or production report server. Figure 5.4 shows the preview view.

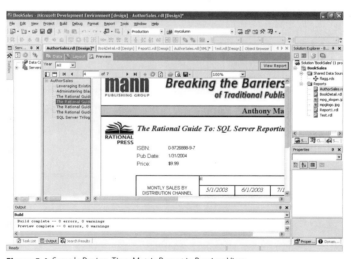

Figure 5.4: Sample Design-Time Matrix Report in Preview View.

The majority of your time spent in creating reports will be in the layout view. This is where you specify the fields on the report, the properties for those fields, the groupings, the types of objects to appear on the report, the formatting and programming of your report, and additional interactivity. Customizing reports is discussed in Chapter 6, while adding interactivity is shown in Chapter 7.

Creating an Empty Report

If you don't use the Report Wizard, you can create an empty report and manually specify every detail. If this is what you want to do, you can create an empty report by following these simple steps:

1   Right-click the **Reports** folder in the Solution Explorer pane.

2   Click the **AddNew Item** menu. You will see a choice of types of items to add to your report project.

3   Click the **Report** template.

4   Give your report a file name. Report files have an **RDL** file extension.

5   Click the **Open** button. Your new, empty report is created.

Report Elements

You can manually add report elements to your reports, even if you choose to create your reports with the Report Wizard. You can add report elements by selecting the desired tool in the **Report Items** tab of the Visual Studio .NET toolbox, as shown in Figure 5.5.

You can choose from these toolbox items:

Figure 5.5: Report Items Toolbox.

▶ **Pointer** — Allows you to select any object on the screen to adjust its position or properties.

▶ **Textbox** — Places a text box on the screen, which can be used for static text or filled with data retrieved from the database.

▶ **Line** — Places a graphical line on the report as a visual element.

▶ **Table** — Places a region on the report that will display your data in a tabular format. The use of tables is discussed further in Chapters 6 and 7.

▶ **Matrix** — Places a region on your report that will display your data in a cross-tab format. The matrix tool is discussed further in Chapters 6 and 7.

▶ **Rectangle** — Places a graphical rectangle on the report to enhance the visual appeal of your report. This is most commonly used to group items together or to control how items are arranged when other items around them expand with data.

▶ **List** — Places a list of data on your report. A list is an alternative to a table or a matrix.

▶ **Image** — Places a graphical image on your report. Images are shown in more detail later in this chapter in the section "Using Images."

▶ **Subreport** — Places another report within your report. The Subreport tool is covered later in this chapter in the section "Including Subreports."

▶ **Chart** — Places a graphical chart or graph on your reports. The chart tool is covered later in this chapter in the section "Displaying Charts."

All of these tools have "drag-and-drop" functionality, so you can drag the tool from the tool palette and drop it onto the work surface of the report. The report must be in layout view to use the tools.

Using Images

To use images on your report, you use the image tool in the Report Items toolbox. When you drag and drop it onto your report work surface, the Image Wizard automatically pops up. The wizard guides you through the options of how to handle images. You must specify the image's source location from these options:

▶ **Embedded** — Embeds the image into the report itself.

▶ **Project** — Embeds the image into the project so other reports can use it.

▶ **Database** — Uses an image stored in a database. To use this option, you must have a data set that returns the image.

To use the wizard, follow these steps:

1   Make sure the **Layout** tab is selected.

2   Drag and drop the image tool onto the work surface.

3   The **Welcome** screen appears. Click **Next** to begin using the wizard.

4   Select the source location for the image — **Embedded**, **Project**, or **Database**. Click **Next** to move to the next step.

5   Choose the image. If you selected **Embedded** or **Project**, you are prompted to locate the file when you click the **New Image** button. If you selected **Database** as the image type, then you must select the

Dataset, **Image field**, and **Mime type** for the image. The **Dataset** is the query that returns the **Image field** of the image. The **Mime type** is the type of image that is stored in the database, such as **GIF**, **JPG**, or **BMP**. Click **Next** when you are ready to continue.

Tech Tip:

It can be useful to store images in the database if the image displayed on the page is dependent upon other field values.

FREE *Bonus:*

If you register this book on the web, you can download a free utility that you can use to manage images in your databases.

6   Click **Finish** to insert the image.

Including Subreports

Subreports are an outstanding feature of SQL Server Reporting Services. A *subreport* is just as it sounds. It's a report within a report. To use the subreport tool, you must have already created a report using the steps outlined in this chapter. Once you save your report, it will become available to any report in the project as a subreport. In other words, suppose you have a report called **Author Royalties**, which reports all sales and royalties for the current year. It might be useful to see a subreport in a small region of the main report that displays the prior year's figures as well. The primary reason for using a subreport is if you have already created another report and you wish to reuse it. You get tremendous return on investment (ROI) if you reuse your existing reports by including them as subreports.

Here's how to include a subreport in a report:

1   Make sure the **Layout** tab is selected.

2   Drag and drop the subreport tool onto the work surface.

3   Open the **Properties** window by pressing the **F4** key.

4   Change the **ReportName** property by selecting the desired report from the dropdown list. You will see a list of all reports in the project, except for the current report.

5   Test your report by clicking the **Preview** tab.

Displaying Charts

A chart is a great way to add useful and visually appealing data to your reports. The chart tool can display data in a wide variety of formats. By default, this tool displays a bar chart. However, you can choose any of these types of charts and graphs with the same tool:

► Column

► Bar

► Area

► Line

► Pie

► Doughnut

► Scatter

► Bubble

► Stock

To display a chart, follow these steps:

1   Make sure the **Layout** tab is selected.

2   Drag and drop the chart tool onto the work surface.

3   Open the **Properties** window by pressing the **F4** key.

4   (Optional) Change the **DataSetName** property by selecting the desired report from the dropdown list. The dataset is where you will retrieve fields that will be placed on the chart.

5   Choose the desired chart type by right-clicking anywhere in the chart region and selecting the **Chart Type** menu.

6   Double-click anywhere in the graph part of the chart tool. This will display data regions needed by the chart tool. Drag and drop the fields that are to be used in the chart into the appropriate area of the control. These regions are shown in Figure 5.6.

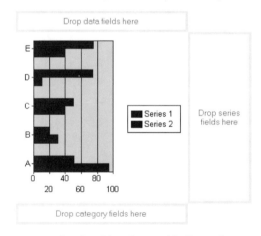

Figure 5.6: Drag/Drop Editing Regions of the Chart tool.

Depending on the type of chart needed in the Chart tool, you will have to specify data fields to display in the chart. At a minimum, the chart tool expects two different fields — data fields and series fields. *Data fields* are those fields that comprise the values in the chart. *Series fields* are those fields that determine the next set of values in a series of values.

7 Drag and drop data fields and series fields onto your chart control.

8 Test your report by clicking the **Preview** tab.

Summary

When you create reports with SQL Server Reporting Services, you do so inside Visual Studio .NET, version 2003 and later. After you install the client-side components from the installation CD, you will be able to create reporting projects and reports within those projects the same way you create any other project that targets a Microsoft platform — by using the familiar Visual Studio .NET environment.

This chapter showed you how to use Visual Studio .NET 2003 to create a new project, create reports within those projects, add elements to your report from the toolbox, and how to configure those elements. These are simple concepts to grasp, but very important to understand as you read through the rest of this book.

Chapter 6

Customizing Reports

The ability to highly customize reports is one of the greatest strengths of SQL Server Reporting Services. Report customization is ultimately stored in the Report Definition Language file (RDL), Using Visual Studio .NET 2003 or later makes customizing reports as simple as dragging and dropping, specifying properties, and entering formulas. If you are familiar with Visual Studio .NET (any version), you know how the development environment aids in high productivity and very fast development. Customizing your reports is just as easy. You can create customized reports in minutes! This chapter gives an overview of how to customize your reports.

Chapter 5 discussed how to use Visual Studio .NET 2003 to create reporting projects. It also discussed which tools are available in the tool palette. This chapter builds upon Chapter 5 for a discussion of how to use the Visual Studio .NET 2003 IDE to customize reports.

Expressions

It is critical that you understand how to use expressions in the report designer. *Expressions* are the syntax used to manipulate data and formatting within your reports. Expressions must be written in the Visual Basic .NET language.

There are five object collections that are available for use in your expressions. These are intrinsic objects implemented as collections that are always available in your reports and are evaluated at runtime:

▶ **Fields** — Fields in the current dataset.

▶ **Globals** — Variables that affect report metrics and the server which is running the report.

▶ **Parameters** — Defined parameters for a report.

▶ **ReportItems** — All text boxes that exist on the report.

▶ **User** — Information about the user running the report.

To help you understand what properties are available in these collections, refer to Table 6.1.

COLLECTION	PROPERTY	DESCRIPTION
Fields	IsMissing	**True** if the property does not exist in the data set.
Fields	Value	The actual value of the specified field.
Globals	ExecutionTime	Timestamp when the report began processing.
Globals	PageNumber	The current page number as evaluated during report processing.
Globals	ReportFolder	The folder on the report server that contains the report.
Globals	ReportName	The name of the running report.
Globals	ReportServerUrl	The URL of the server running the report.
Globals	TotalPages	The total number of pages in the report.
Parameters	Label	The label of the parameter, such as **Washington**.
Parameters	Value	The actual value for the parameter, such as **WA**.
ReportItems	Value	The actual value of the referenced text box.
User	Language	The ID of the language used in the report, such as **en-US** for US English.
User	UserID	The UserID of the current user running the report. The UserID will be the ID used to log into the network or resource, including the domain name, if applicable.

Table 6.1: SQL Server Reporting Services Intrinsic Collections and Properties.

Using any of the collections and properties in Table 6.1 requires this syntax:

Example 1

SYNTAX

```
=<<Collection>>!<<Property>>
```

EXAMPLE

```
=User!Language
```

Example 2

SYNTAX

```
=<<Collection>>!<<Item>>.<<Property>>
```

EXAMPLE

```
=Fields!DivisionID.Value
```

As long as you understand how to access the intrinsic collections, you can use typical Visual Basic .NET expressions such as concatenations, arithmetic and aggregation operations, and more.

Expressions can be assigned to almost any report item property. The most common property that you will assign is **Value**. You can assign the value by typing the desired expression in the properties window, or by using the Expression Builder. The *Expression Builder* is a small pop-up window that allows you to either type an expression or select an object from the collections shown in Table 6.1. The Expression Builder can be invoked from virtually any report item in the IDE. To bring up the Expression Builder, select the desired report item property for which you will build the expression. You'll see a dropdown list of possible values. The first possible value is named **<Expression...>**. Click this option to bring up the Expression Builder, as shown in Figure 6.1.

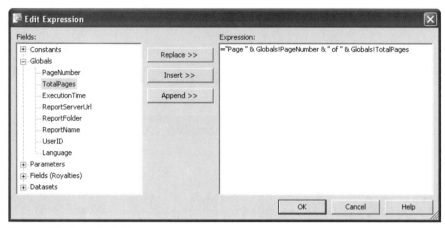

Figure 6.1: The Expression Builder.

Notice in Figure 6.1, the expression contained in the **Expression** box shows a combination of global variables and string literals. The expression is evaluated at runtime to yield a result that is displayed in the text box, such as Page 1 of 5

Formatting

You can format the fields on your report by specifying values for many report item properties, such as (but not limited to):

► **BackgroundColor**

► **Color**

► **Direction**

► **FontWeight**

► **FontSize**

► **Format**

To set these values, you can either enter the required value for the property, or enter an expression using the Expression Builder. The required value is specific to the property. For example, the color-related properties require either the name of the color, such as "Black" or "Red," or their hexadecimal equivalents. Hexadecimal equivalents are comprised of six individual numbers, such as "#000000" for black and "ff000" for red. Similarly, changing the **FontSize** property requires the exact font size, such as "10pt" or "12pt."

If you know what type of values a property expects, you can assign them conditionally at runtime using the **IIF** statement, which follows this syntax:

SYNTAX
```
=IIF(<<Collection>>!<<Property>>.Value <<Condition>> <<Test_Value>>,
<<True_Value>>, <<False_Value>>)
```

Variables:

▶   <<Collection>> is the name of the collection from Table 6.1.

▶   <<Property>> is the name of the property from Table 6.1.

▶   <<Condition>> is the Visual Basic .NET condition that you wish to test with, such as "<" for less than, ">" for greater than, and "<>" for not equal to.

▶   <<Test_Value>> is the value you wish to test with the <Condition>.

▶   <<True_Value>> is the resulting value that will be used if the test evaluates to **True**.

▶   <<False_Value>> is the resulting value that will be used if the test evaluates to **False**.

EXAMPLE
```
=IIF(Fields!Sales.Value < 0, "18pt", "10pt")
```

This example is the expression assigned to the **FontSize** property. It makes the font size 18 points if the value in the **Sales** field is less than zero. Otherwise, a font size of 10 points is used.

Headers and Footers

As briefly explained in Chapter 3, headers and footers are a very important part of your report design. Headers and footers can contain some of the same elements as the body of your report, such as text boxes and graphic elements. However, these elements cannot be included in headers and footers:

►   **Matrix**

►   **Table**

►   **List**

►   **Subreport**

►   **Chart**

These elements are data-specific and must consider how data is grouped on the page, so including these elements in the header or footer will make grouping impossible. Grouping is always specified in the report body. Additionally, you can not refer to the **Fields** collection in a header or footer. You must use the **ReportItems** collection instead.

To include either a header or footer on the report, simply click the **Report** ➪ **Page Header** or **Report** ➪ **Page Footer** menus. You'll see these regions created in the **Layout** view, which is shown in Figure 6.2.

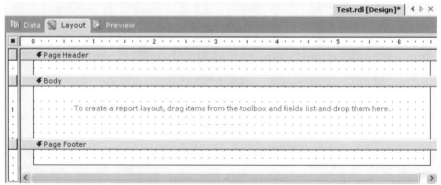

Figure 6.2: Including Headers and Footers.

Programmability

Microsoft implemented SQL Server Reporting Services as a Web Service, so you can access virtually any aspect of the reporting server programmatically. This includes server configurations, reports, and more. A *Web Service* is a specification for integrating applications and accessing a defined programming interface using standard Internet protocols.

Just like any other object that you use in any Visual Studio .NET project (such as a Windows Application, ASP .NET Web, or ASP .NET Web Service), the interface of the object determines the properties, methods, and events that you can access within your programs. Before you can do any programming with the reporting services objects, you must understand their interfaces. It is impossible to discuss in this short book all of the properties, methods, and events associated with the SQL Server Reporting Services Web Service, but as a pointer, you can search the online help for "ReportingService Class" or use the Object Browser inside Visual Studio .NET 2003. For more information about using the Object Browser, consult the Visual Studio .NET 2003 online help.

Before you can programmatically access any SQL Server Reporting Services object, you must set a Web Reference to the location of your report server. To set a Web Reference, follow these steps:

1   Open Visual Studio .NET 2003 and create a new **Windows Application** or **ASP .NET Web Application** project.

2   Right-click the name of your project in the Solution Explorer window.

3   Click the **Add Web Reference** menu.

4   In the **Add Web Reference** dialog box that is presented, enter the URL of your reporting server Web Service. The URL will follow this general syntax:

SYNTAX

```
http://<<Server>>/<<Report_Server>>/reportservice.asmx?wsdl
```

Variables:

- <<Server>> is the name of your report server. This can be either an internal name or an external name accessible over the Internet.

- <<Report_Server>> is the name of the reporting server site that hosts the Web Service. You specified this location when you installed SQL Server Reporting Services. This web site name is **ReportServer** by default.

EXAMPLE

```
http://trapper/ReportServer/reportservice.asmx?wsdl
```

This example sets a Web Reference to an internal server named **trapper** using the default web server location.

5   Click the **Go** button. The system will attempt to locate the Web Service. If it does find the Web Service, the **Add Reference** button will become enabled. This is shown in Figure 6.3.

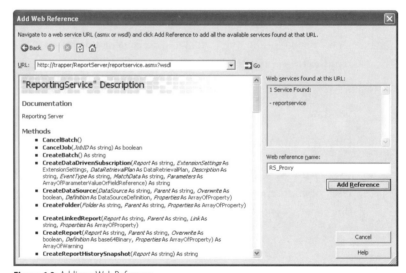

Figure 6.3: Adding a Web Reference.

6   Change the Web Reference name to something that makes more
     sense to use in your code, such as **RS_Proxy**.

7   Click the **Add Reference** button. The new Web Reference will be
     added to your Visual Studio .NET project. You can now access all
     aspects of the report server via the Web Service proxy.

It is not possible to show how to programmatically manage all aspects of your
reports and reporting server, but there are a few basics that you must understand.
To help illustrate some basic points, refer to Figure 6.4, which is used in the
following discussion.

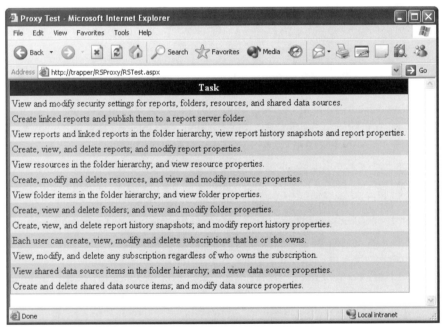

Figure 6.4: Sample Web Service Application.

The example shown in Figure 6.4 queries the report server using the Web
Reference that was set earlier in this chapter. The report server is queried by
using the **ListTasks** method of the Web Service, building a .NET data table
object, and binding that object to a data grid. The example was built using the
Visual Basic .NET Language, with code shown in Listing 6.1.

```
'create an instance of the reporting service proxy
Dim MyRS As New RS_Proxy.ReportingService

'set default security credentials
MyRS.Credentials =
System.Net.CredentialCache.DefaultCredentials

'get a list of tasks
Dim tsk As RS_Proxy.Task() = MyRS.ListTasks

'create a data table from the retrieved tasks
RSGrid.DataSource = CreateDataTable(tsk)

'bind the grid
RSGrid.DataBind()
```

Listing 6.1: Visual Basic .NET Code for Sample Web Service Application.

In Listing 6.1, a lot of work is being done with only a few lines of code. The most important line of code is the first line, where a variable, **myRS**, is declared as being of the type **RS_Proxy.ReportingService**. **RS_Proxy** was the name of the Web Service reference that you specified in the section "Programmability," earlier in this chapter. The next line of code sets the security credentials to those of the cached or already logged-in user. This gives the Web Service a security context. If you don't set the security context, subsequent calls to the Web Service will fail. The third line of code creates an object, **tsk**, of type **Task**. In the same line of code, it assigns the **tsk** object the list of tasks that are returned by the **ListTasks** method of the Web Service. **ListTasks** returns all item-level tasks. Alternatively, you can call the **ListSystemTasks** method to return only system-level tasks. Tasks are discussed in Chapter 9. The last two lines of code assign the list of tasks to a data grid that is automatically bound. The code in the **CreateDataTable** function is not shown in this chapter, but can be downloaded on the web.

Summary

You have virtually unlimited possibilities in customizing your reports. Not only can you include expressions in most of the properties for Reporting Services objects, but you can also access most reporting services objects programmatically from a Visual Studio .NET project. Using Visual Studio .NET and the SQL Server Reporting Services Web Service interface, you can actually create an application similar to Report Manager.

Chapter 7

Adding
Interactivity

In Chapter 6, you learned how you can customize your reports by adding Visual Basic .NET expressions to customize data and formatting. This chapter takes those concepts further and allows you to add interactivity to your reports. *Interactivity* refers to adding functionality to your report to allow users themselves to interact with the report at runtime to display data the way they wish to view it.

Parameters

Parameters are a way to allow users to filter the data displayed on a report. Parameters are a great way to add interactivity to your reports by allowing users to limit the data on the report to exactly what they want to see. There are two types of parameters: data set and report. Data set parameters affect the rows of data returned by the data set and report parameters are used to prompt the user for input.

Data set parameters are used to provide variable assignments to stored procedures that accept parameters. Suppose you have the stored procedure with two parameters defined in Listing 7.1.

```
CREATE PROCEDURE usp_ReportRoyalties
    @Year as integer = NULL,
    @AuthorID as integer = NULL
AS
    ---STATEMENTS GO HERE
GO
```

Listing 7.1: Sample Stored Procedure Showing Parameters.

When you create a data set using the stored procedure shown in Listing 7.1, SQL Server Reporting Services automatically creates two different types of parameters — data set and report. Data set parameters are created with the same two names declared inside the stored procedure in Listing 7.1 — **@Year** and **@AuthorID**. Report parameters are also created with the names **Year** and **AuthorID**.

Verifying Data Set Parameters

Data set parameters can be verified by editing the data set and clicking the **Parameters** tab. Editing a data set is shown in Chapter 4.

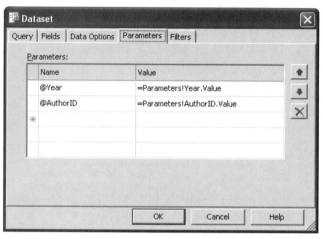

Figure 7.1: Verifying Data Set Parameters.

Notice in Figure 7.1 that the **Name** column lists all parameters as defined in the stored procedure that makes up the data set. They are all, by default, assigned to parameters in the **Value** column with the same name. Any item in the **Parameters** collection will automatically prompt the user for a value when the report is run.

Verifying Report Parameters

To verify report parameters, follow these steps:

1   Open your project in Visual Studio .NET 2003.

2   Open the desired report within the project.

3   Select the **Layout** tab.

4   Click the **Report** ⇨ **Report Parameters** menu. This brings up the
      Report Parameters screen, as shown in Figure 7.2.

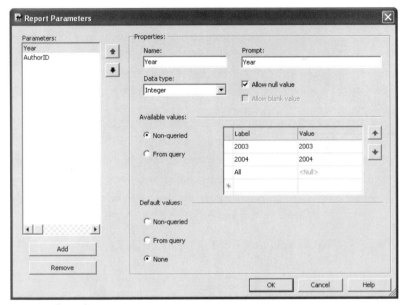

Figure 7.2: Report Parameters.

5   For each selected parameter, you can fill in these properties:

- **Name** — The name of the parameter as it is referred to in the
  report **Parameters** collection.

- **Prompt** — The label shown on the screen to prompt the user
  for input.

- **Data type** — The data type of the selected parameter. The data
  type is retrieved from the stored procedure when the data set is
  created. The only data types allowed are **Boolean**, **DateTime**,
  Integer, **Float**, and **String**.

- **Allow null value** — This option allows null (or missing)
  values for a parameter.

- **Allow blank value** — This option allows an empty string, or blank value. This option is only enabled for a **String** data type.

- **Available values** — This option allows you to indicate how the system will retrieve a list of possible values for the selected parameter. These possible values will be used to provide the user with a dropdown list of choices when the report runs. Choose from these options:

  - **Non-queried** — Default option that provides static choices to the user, such as **Yes** and **No**. If you provide a list of values, you must specify both **Label** and **Value** for each item in the list. The **Label** is the text that appears on the screen in the dropdown list, while **Value** is the value used by the system when the **Label** is selected.

  - **From query** — Option to retrieve a list of values from the database.

- **Default values** — Allows you to specify the value that appears by default for the selected parameter. Select from these options:

  - **Non-queried** — Option that allows you to specify the default value in an expression.

  - **From query** — Option that allows you to indicate a data set and value field that retrieves the default parameter value from the database.

  - **None** — Option that indicates no default value will be provided to the user.

6 Click the **OK** button to save your changes and close the screen.

Filters

A *filter* is another way to limit data processed by a report. A filter is applied to a query after it is returned from the database, so it is not the same as limiting data using parameters or a SQL **WHERE** clause in the data set definition. In other words, all data is returned from the query and then the filter is applied inside the report before it is rendered.

Filters can be applied to data sets, data regions (matrix or table), and also to groups inside a table, matrix, list, or chart. Filters are applied in much the same way for all objects. So, as an example, here's how you apply a filter to a data set:

1   Open your project in Visual Studio .NET 2003.

2   Open the desired report.

3   Select the **Data** tab.

4   Click the Ellipsis (**...**) button to edit the data set.

5   Click the **Filters** tab, which is shown in Figure 7.3.

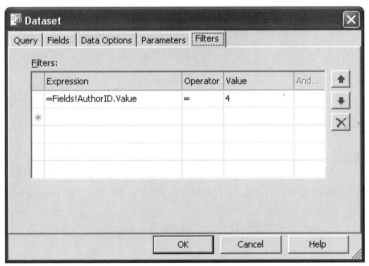

Figure 7.3: Report Filters.

6   There are only four fields on this screen that you must fill in. These fields are used to specify test conditions that, if true, will limit the data to only the values that pass the test. You can specify multiple tests, but each individual test condition will be considered an **and** or an **or** operation with other tests. Conditions are entered as separate rows in the grid. An **and** condition will be applied for condition 1 and condition 2 and condition 3, etc. An **or** condition will be applied for condition 1 or condition 2, etc. If different expressions are on two consecutive lines, an automatic **and** condition will be applied. On the other hand, if two different expressions exist on consecutive lines, an automatic **or** condition will be applied. You can specify your test conditions with these fields:

- **Expression** — The field or expression to test for.

- **Operator** — The conditional operator to use in the test.

- **Value** — The value to test the **Expression** field with.

- **And** — This field is disabled and will follow the automatic rules previously mentioned. It is used as a visual indication of how the conditions specified in two consecutive rows will be handled.

7   Click the **OK** button to save your changes.

Document Map

A *document map* is a table of contents that is automatically generated when a report is rendered in an HTML, PDF, or Excel format. However, you have control over how the document map is displayed. Before continuing, refer to Figure 7.4, which shows a rendered report with a document map displayed. The document map can be toggled on and off with the document map button.

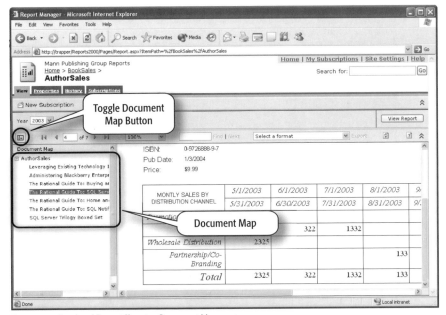

Figure 7.4: Rendered Report Showing Document Map.

The value that appears in the document map is called a *document map label*. Document map labels may be specified in most report items, such as text boxes, matrixes, and tables. You'll notice that in Figure 7.4, the labels shown in the document map are generated from the database (because they are actual titles of books). That is because document map labels can be expressions, such as the value of a text box. Document maps are automatically generated when one or more document map labels are specified in a report. To add document map labels, you can follow this procedure:

1 Open your project in Visual Studio .NET 2003.

2 Open the desired report.

3 Select the **Layout** tab.

4 Open the **Properties** screen by right-clicking the desired object and clicking the **Properties** menu.

5 Click the **Navigation** tab. This brings up the screen shown in Figure 7.5.

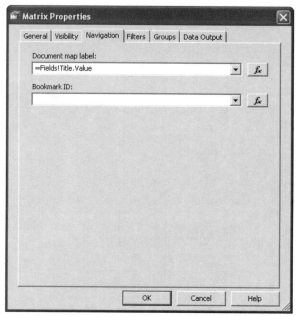

Figure 7.5: Specifying a Document Map Label.

6   Enter the desired expression associated with the document map
     label. In Figure 7.5, the document map label will be the same as the
     Title field coming from the database. The **Value** property of the
     field is resolved at runtime.

7   Click the **OK** button to close the screen.

Bookmarks

Bookmarks are similar in concept to a document map in that they will jump to a
specific area of the screen when clicked. Like document maps, bookmarks jump
to a specific area within a page on a report, but they exist in the report rather than
in a separate section, the way a document map is. You can assign bookmarks in
much the same way as you assigned document map labels.

There are two parts to a bookmark. The first is the area of the screen that contains a bookmark ID. This is a unique string assigned to a specific item on the screen. The second part of a bookmark is the area of the screen that you click to jump to the assigned bookmark ID. Both of these items must be configured for the bookmark to function.

For example, suppose you have a text box at the bottom of the report, named **GrandTotal**. You might assign the **GrandTotal** text box a unique bookmark ID (using the **Bookmark** property), such as **BKM_Total**. Then, you create a link at the top of the screen that, when clicked, will immediately jump to the **BKM_Total** bookmark by using the **Action** property. The aforementioned link can be either a text box or an image.

Making this happen is simpler than it may sound. Here's how you do it:

1   Open your project in Visual Studio .NET 2003.

2   Open the desired report.

3   Select the **Layout** tab.

4   Click the field that is to have the bookmark assigned.

5   Press the **F4** key to bring up the **Properties** window.

6   Enter a unique string value into the **Bookmark** property to identify the bookmark, like this (note the equals sign and the quotation marks): `="BKM _ Total"`

7   Add an image or text box control onto the report and ensure it is selected.

8   Press the **F4** key to bring up the **Properties** window.

9   Next to the **Action** property, click the ellipsis (**...**) button to show the **Action** dialog box in Figure 7.6.

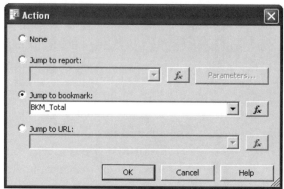

Figure 7.6: Specifying Action Properties.

10   Click the **Jump to bookmark** option.

11   Enter the same bookmark as you did in step 5.

12   Click **OK** to save your changes and close the dialog box.

13   Run your report and click the image or text box that you placed
     at the top of the report and watch the report jump to the specified
     location.

Drillthrough

Drillthrough is a term used to describe the action of clicking on an area of a
report (Report 1) to run another report (Report 2) to show additional details. The
only way this can work is if Report 1 can pass parameters to Report 2 that are
specific to the area clicked in Report 1.

Here is an example of a drillthrough scenario. Suppose you have a report, called
AuthorSales, which displays the sales figures by author by book for the desired
year. This is shown in Figure 7.4. It can be quite useful to allow the user to click
on the title of the book to run another report, called **BookDetail**, to display details
about the book, such as book price, size, publication date, names of editors, and
more. For the **BookDetail** report to display these items for a specific book, it
must be configured with a **BookID** parameter to select data for a specific book.
Once you have both reports working as self-contained units, you are ready to
configure the drillthrough action.

To configure drillthrough interactivity in your reports, follow these steps:

1   Open your project in Visual Studio .NET 2003.

2   Open the report that you wish to use as a drillthrough report, such as **AuthorSales**.

3   Select the **Layout** tab.

4   Click the field that is to have the bookmark assigned.

5   Press the **F4** key to bring up the **Properties** window.

6   Next to the **Action** property, click the ellipsis (**...**) button to show the **Action** dialog box in Figure 7.6.

7   Click the **Jump to report** option.

8   From the dropdown list, click the report name that is the target of the drillthrough. To continue with the example, you would choose the **BookDetail** report.

9   Click the **Parameters** button. This brings up the dialog box shown in Figure 7.7.

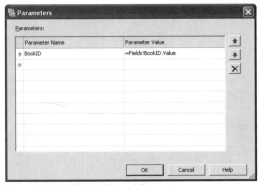

Figure 7.7: Specifying Drillthrough Parameters.

10   In the **Parameter Name** column, select from the dropdown list the parameter name from the target report you wish to assign. Following our example, you would choose the **BookID** parameter for the previously selected **BookDetail** report.

11   In the **Parameter Value** column, select or enter the expression that
     supplies the value to the parameter. In the preceding example, that
     field is called **BookID**, so the full expression is:

     ```
     =Fields!BookID.Value
     ```

12   Click the **OK** button to close the **Parameters** dialog box.

13   Click the **OK** button to close the **Action** dialog box.

Drilldown

Drilldown allows a user to drill further into a report to show more detail. An
example of a drilldown report would be showing book sales on an annual basis,
but allowing the user to interactively drilldown into the report to show book sales
by quarter or month. A user knows about drilldown capabilities being available
on a report because they will see the familiar **+** and **-** signs. This is similar to the
way you would view files in the Windows Explorer. In other words, if you want
to see the files inside a folder (or drilldown), you click the **+** sign. To collapse the
details, you would click the **-** sign. Figure 7.8 shows an example of a collapsed
report to allow drilldown capabilities.

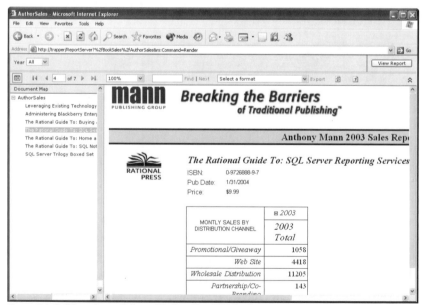

Figure 7.8: Drilldown Report Collapsed To Show Year 2003 Totals.

The ability to automatically include drilldown capabilities and to show or hide sections or fields on a report is known as *visibility*. If you wish to automatically control the drilldown capabilities inside a matrix, you must alter the properties of the matrix grouping, not individual rows or text boxes within the matrix. To control the drilldown and visibility properties on report fields, simply follow this procedure:

1   Inside the matrix, select the desired heading for which you want to control visibility.

2   Bring up the **Editing and Sorting Properties** dialog box by right-clicking the matrix object and then clicking the **Edit Group** menu.

3   Click the **Visibility** tab. You'll see the dialog box shown in Figure 7.9.

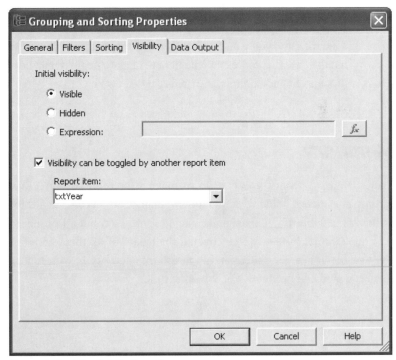

Figure 7.9: Specifying Visibility Properties.

4   Select the desired **Initial visibility** option:

- **Visible** — Field is visible when the report loads.

- **Hidden** — Field is hidden when the report loads.

- **Expression** — Any valid expression can control the visibility of the field. For example, you may want the visibility to be hidden if there are no sales for a year, but visible if there are sales.

5   Check the **Visibility can be toggled by another report item** option if you want to automatically generate drilldown capability, based on another item. This option allows you to specify another report item that controls visibility. In Figure 7.8, the **Year** field controls the visibility of the grouping on the report. When you specify that another report item controls visibility, you automatically see the **+** and **-** navigational links on the report to handle drilldown capabilities. Therefore, to enable this functionality, you would select from the **Report item** dropdown list the field that represents the item to click to begin the drilldown process. In our example, the field is called **txtYear**.

6   Click the **OK** button to save your changes.

Summary

There are many things you can do to make your reports interactive, such as adding parameters, filters, a document map, bookmarks, drillthrough, and drilldown capabilities. This sounds like a lot of work, but all of these activities are quite simple. In fact, we've covered the basics of all these activities in only a few pages. It is a good idea for you to use interactivity in your reports to keep users engaged and productive at the same time.

Part III

Managing Reports

Chapter 8

Report Processing and Management

There are many options available for processing and managing your reports and your reporting server. Subject to the appropriate security privileges, you can manage how the reports are cached and executed. You can also manage report definition language files (RDL files) and report history. In this chapter, you will learn about these topics and discover the difference between caching and snapshots.

Caching Overview

SQL Server Reporting Services allows for caching reports to ensure that frequent access to the same reports using the same parameters does not require additional processing time. SQL Server Reporting Services stores a copy of the report in a special area of the server, called a *cache*. Then, the report is delivered from the cache, without the need to reprocess the report or waste valuable CPU cycles and memory. The reporting server will cache a copy of the report according to options you set.

SQL Server Reporting Services also allows you to create snapshots of your reports. A snapshot is a close cousin to the cache. However, the main difference between a snapshot and a cache is that a snapshot is usually created on a regular schedule. This allows you to control server resources. A cache is created upon the first running of the report, and also after the cache expires. Additionally, only one snapshot can be stored for each report, whereas a cache may store multiple copies of the report. The caching and snapshot options for a report can be changed by anyone who is assigned to the **Manage Reports** task on a report, such as a **Content Manager** or **Publisher**.

Report Properties

There are numerous report-related properties that you can change. These properties are broken up into a series of individual tabs on the screen. Because these tabs are actually within other tabs, they are referred to as sub-tabs. Once you change the desired values, simply click the **Apply** button to save your changes.

General Properties

There are not many general report properties that you can change (outside of the report definition itself), but you can change the name and description. To do so, follow these simple steps:

1   Open Report Manager in Internet Explorer.

2   Navigate to the desired report.

3   Run the desired report.

4   Click the **Properties** tab.

5   Ensure the **General** sub-tab is clicked, as it will be by default. This brings up the screen shown in Figure 8.1.

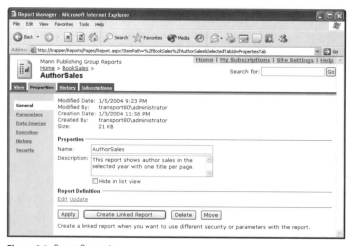

Figure 8.1: Report Properties.

6   Enter values for the **Properties** section:

- **Name** — The name of your report. This name will appear everywhere the report listing is displayed, such as within folders, in schedules, and in history. Make sure to name your report something that is applicable to the way it will be used. This field is mandatory.

- **Description** — The description of your report. It is a good idea to give your reports a description, so that users can decide which report to run. This field is optional.

- **Hide in list view** — If checked, this option will ensure that the report is not shown along with the rest of the reports in the folder. It is effectively hidden. Hidden reports are only hidden in the list view of Report Manager. They are always visible in the detail view. The most common reason for hiding reports is that they are drillthrough targets of other reports and are not meant to be used independently.

7   Select options for the **Report Definition** section:

- **Edit** — This link downloads the stored RDL file for the report onto your hard drive. From there, you can open it in whatever tool you have to edit RDL files, such as Visual Studio .NET 2003 or later.

- **Update** — This link allows you to upload an RDL file onto the report server. The RDL file is the definition of the report itself. Another way to get your report definition uploaded to the report server is to deploy it using Visual Studio .NET 2003 or later. Deployment is covered in Chapter 11.

8   Select the desired action by clicking any of these command buttons at the bottom of the screen:

- **Apply** — Accepts and saves your changes.

- **Create Linked Report** — Allows you to create a new report based on the currently selected report, but with different parameter values or properties. This option in effect creates a shortcut to the original report from the new report. You can change parameters or properties of the new report without affecting the original report.

- **Delete** — Deletes the current report.

- **Move** — Moves the current report by prompting you for a new folder location.

Parameters

Parameters are defined in the Report Definition Language (RDL) file. However, you can control the behavior of those parameters on the screen when the report is rendered. To configure properties related to parameters, run the desired report, click the **Properties** tab and then the **Parameters** sub-tab, which is shown in Figure 8.2. One row is displayed for each parameter that is defined in the report.

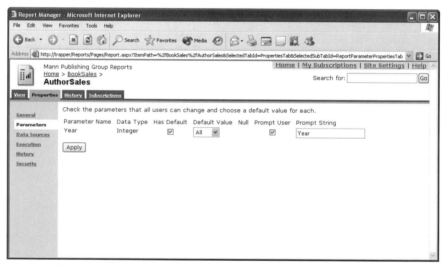

Figure 8.2: Report Parameters.

These parameter properties are available:

▶ **Parameter Name** — The name of the parameter as it is defined in the report. This can only be changed in the RDL file.

▶ **Data Type** — The data type of the parameter as it is defined in the report. This can only be changed in the RDL file.

▶ **Has Default** — Checking this box allows you to specify a default value for the parameter. If all report parameters have default values, the report will be run immediately when the **View** tab is clicked.

▶ **Default Value** — Allows you to specify or enter the default value for the parameter if the **Has Default** property is checked.

▶ **Null** — Checking this box will allow you to specify a null value for parameter. This check box is only visible if the parameter defined in the RDL file allows null values.

▶ **Prompt User** — The option will prompt the user for a value for the parameter. If this option is not checked, the user will have no way to select a value for this parameter. You must supply a value on this screen in the **Default Value** field.

▶ **Prompt String** — The visual prompt for the parameter value that the user sees on the screen. By default, this value is the same as the parameter name itself.

Execution

Execution properties define how the reports are executed, including snapshot and caching configurations. To configure properties related to report execution, run the desired report, click the **Properties** tab and then the **Execution** sub-tab, which is shown in Figure 8.3.

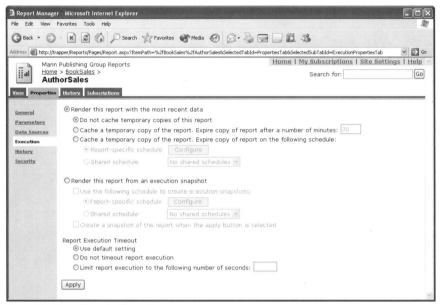

Figure 8.3: Report Execution Properties.

There are multiple options under the **Execution** sub-tab for you to choose how your reports are executed:

► **Render this report with the most recent data** — If you choose this option, you must further choose these caching options:

  • **Do not cache temporary copies of this report** — If chosen, the report will be generated from the data source every time it is run.

  • **Cache a temporary copy of the report** — If chosen, will automatically cache a copy of the report. You can choose to expire the report cache after a certain number of minutes or upon a specific schedule. When the cache is expired, the next run of the report will place it in the cache again.

► **Render this report from an execution snapshot** — If you choose this option, you must choose additional options about how the report server manages report snapshots:

- **Use the following schedule to create execution snapshots** — Will create regular snapshots according to the schedule specified.

- **Create a snapshot of the report when the apply button is selected** — Will create a snapshot immediately upon clicking the **Apply** button on this screen.

> *Note:*
>
> **If you set up your report without choosing this option, all requests for this report will return an error until the snapshot is created at the scheduled time.**

▶ **Report Execution Timeout** — Allows you to specify how long the reports will run before they time out. You can specify these options:

- **Use default setting** — If chosen, the report timeout value will be inherited from the settings on the **Site Settings** web page. This is the option selected by default.

- **Do not timeout report execution** — If chosen, the report will run forever, until it completes execution on its own. This option can potentially block resources and degrade server performance.

- **Limit report execution to the following number of sections** — Allows you to specify how many seconds the report runs before timing out.

History

Another option available to you is to control how the history of the selected report is stored. *History* is a series of report snapshots stored on the server. To configure properties related to report history, run the desired report, click the **Properties** tab and then the **History** sub-tab, which is shown in Figure 8.4.

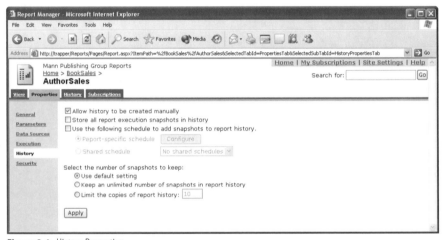

Figure 8.4: History Properties.

There are multiple options under the **History** sub-tab for you to choose how your reports are rendered:

▶ **Allow history to be created manually** — If you choose this option, you can create ad-hoc snapshots (not according to a specified time period) on the **History** tab by clicking the **New Snapshot** button.

▶ **Store all report execution snapshots in history** — Allows report snapshots to be stored in the database history. These reports can be viewed on the **History** tab.

▶ **Use the following schedule to add snapshots to report history** — If checked, the report server will automatically add report snapshots to history, according to the specified schedule.

▶ **Select the number of snapshots to keep** — To conserve disk space, you can limit the number of snapshots stored in history, as follows:

- **Use default setting** — If chosen, the number of snapshots to retain in history will be inherited from the settings on the **Site Settings** web page. This is the default option.

- **Keep an unlimited number of snapshots in report history** — If chosen, an unlimited number of reports will be stored in history. The number of reports is limited solely by the amount of disk space in the report server database.

- **Limit the copies of report history** — Allows you to specify the number of reports that are kept in history before they are deleted in rotation.

Summary

There are lots of options available to you for controlling the properties of your deployed reports. Not only can you manage the parameters of a report using Report Manager, you can update your report definition as well. Additionally, there are numerous options that affect the creation and retention of your report snapshots and cache. Creating snapshots and caching your reports is a very effective and important strategy in managing performance, but you must consider your options very carefully. If you don't consider your options, you might run out of system resources or negatively impact performance.

Chapter 9

Report
Security

Like all Microsoft applications, SQL Server Reporting Services was designed from the ground up with security in mind. *Security* refers to the prevention of unauthorized activity in all aspects of your reporting server. Security in SQL Server Reporting Services is implemented using a role-based model. A *role-based* model is an approach to security in which a job function, known as a *role*, is assigned specific privileges throughout the system. Privileges are also known as *tasks*. Then, individual users or groups of users are assigned to those roles. For example, members of the **Sales** group might be assigned to a **Browser** role that has privileges to only view and subscribe to reports in the **SalesReports** folder, but not to create reports in any folder.

The roles in SQL Server Reporting Services are designed to control who has access to report server features, but they do not secure the data itself. There are a variety of ways to secure data and credentials, such as encryption, restricting access to a data source, and more. You can either use the predefined roles that are installed with SQL Server Reporting Services or create your own custom roles. You assign tasks to roles and associate users to roles. This chapter shows you how to use role-based security to protect your reports and reporting server.

To illustrate another example, consider the following scenario. Suppose your company maintains tight controls over security. You may want to ensure that certain users can view reports, but not subscribe to them. Preventing report subscription can not only save on system resources, but it can prevent the possibility of subscribers forwarding the report to someone who is not authorized to see it. In this case, you might want to create a custom role called **ViewOnly**, and assign the appropriate tasks to that role.

Predefined Roles

There are six predefined roles that are created when you install SQL Server Reporting Services. These roles group the most typical sets of tasks for quick assignment to users. Furthermore, predefined roles are defined into two categories: item-level roles and system-level roles.

Item-level roles are assigned tasks that affect individual items, such as reports, folders, and resources. These item-level roles are predefined:

► **Browser** — Run reports and navigate the folder structure on the reporting server.

► **Content Manager** — Manage folders and storage of content on the reporting server, but not publish content.

► **Publisher** — Publish content to a folder on the reporting server.

► **My Reports** — The default role used for the **My Reports** folder.

System-level roles are assigned tasks that affect the entire reporting server, instead of individual items and folders. These system-level roles are predefined:

► **System Administrator** — Perform any function on the reporting server.

► **System User** — View basic server information, such as shared jobs.

Predefined roles are an excellent way to quickly handle security by pre-grouping known tasks with job functions that are likely to take place in your organization. You can, however, modify the predefined roles or even create new ones, as shown throughout this chapter.

Tasks

Before you completely understand role-based security, you need to know that the lowest-level security mechanism is called a task. Roles are a way to group tasks together and assign them to users. Table 9.1 illustrates the relationship between roles and tasks by showing all preconfigured roles and tasks in SQL Server Reporting Services.

TASKS		ROLES					
Task	Task-Level	Browser	Content Manager	My Reports	Publisher	System Admin	System User
Create linked reports	Item		■	■	■		
Generate events	System						
Manage all subscriptions	Item		■				
Manage data sources	Item		■	■	■		
Manage folders	Item		■	■	■		
Manage individual subscriptions	Item	■	■	■			
Manage jobs	System					■	
Manage report history	Item		■	■			
Manage report server properties	System					■	
Manage report server security	System					■	
Manage reports	Item		■	■	■		
Manage resources	Item		■	■	■		
Manage roles	System					■	
Manage shared schedules	System					■	
Set security for individual items	Item		■				
View data sources	Item		■	■			
View folders	Item	■	■	■			
View report server properties	System						■
View reports	Item	■	■	■			
View resources	Item	■	■	■			
View shared schedules	System						■

Table 9.1: Default Roles and Tasks.

Assigning Tasks to Roles

Whether you use predefined roles or define your own roles, you assign tasks to those roles the same way. Here's how:

1   Login to your network as a user assigned to the **System Administrator** role.

2   Open Report Manager in Internet Explorer.

3   Click the **Site Settings** link.

4   In the Security area of the screen, you'll notice three separate, security-related links. These are shown in Figure 9.1.

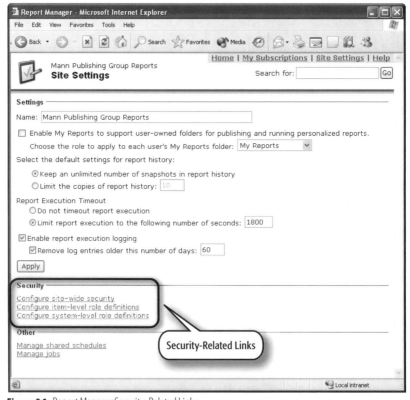

Figure 9.1: Report Manager Security-Related Links.

5   Click either the **Configure item-level role definitions** link or the
    Configure system-level role definitions link. You'll see a list of
    roles associated with the link chosen, as shown in Figure 9.2.

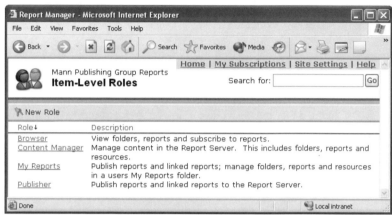

Figure 9.2: Viewing Item-Level Roles.

6   To edit a role, simply click its link. To add a new role, click the **New
    Role** button. Either way, you will see the screen shown in Figure
    9.3.

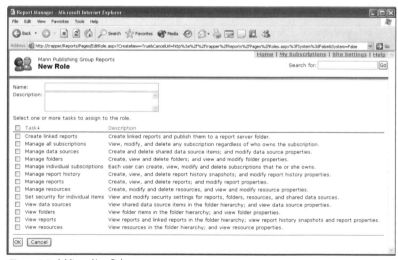

Figure 9.3: Adding a New Role.

7 Enter or change the description assigned to the selected role.

8 If you are adding a new role, you must also give it a name. This name will be used throughout the security subsystem when assigning tasks, users, and groups.

9 Check the boxes for each task that is to be associated with the selected role. If there is no check mark in the column, then the task is not associated with the role.

10 Click the **OK** button to save your changes, **Cancel** to discard your changes, **Delete** to delete the selected role, or **Copy** to copy all tasks to a new role.

> *Note:*
>
> System-level roles are assigned the same way, except that the tasks available for assignment to the role are different. See Table 9.1 for a list of System-level tasks.

Assigning Users and Groups

Once you have assigned tasks to roles, you can assign users or groups of users to those roles. You will use one of two methods to assign users to roles, depending on whether you wish to assign a user to a server-level role or an item-level role.

System Roles

A system role is one that is assigned to system-level tasks. To assign users and groups to system roles, follow these simple steps:

1 Open Report Manager in Internet Explorer.

2 Click the **Site Settings** link.

3 Click the **Configure site-wide security** link. You'll see a list of groups and users and the role(s) they are associated with. This is shown in Figure 9.4.

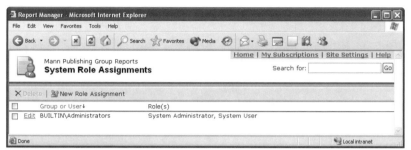

Figure 9.4: System Role Assignments.

4   To edit the role assignments, simply click the **Edit** link next to the desired role. To add a new role assignment, click the **New Role Assignment** button. Either way, you will see the screen shown in Figure 9.5.

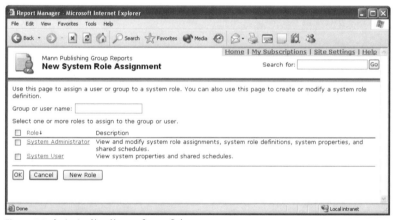

Figure 9.5: Assigning New Users to System Roles.

5   If you are adding a new assignment, enter the name of the new user or group in the **Group or user name** text box. Use this format for entering the user or group:

Local Account:

SYNTAX
```
<<user_or_group>>
```

EXAMPLE
```
Sales
```

Domain Account:

SYNTAX
```
<<domain>>\<<user_or_group>>
```

EXAMPLE
```
MannPub\Sales
```

6   If you are editing an assignment, click the **Apply** button to save your changes or **Cancel** to discard your changes. Click the **New Role** button to assign a new system-level role and bring up the screen shown in Figure 9.3. You can also click the **Delete Role Assignment** button to remove the current role assignment from the system. This will not delete the system role, only the assignment to the user or group.

7   If you are adding a new assignment, click the **OK** button to save your changes or **Cancel** to discard your changes. Click the **New Role** button to assign a new system-level role and bring up the screen shown in Figure 9.3. The security account that you enter will be validated before the role assignment is saved.

By default, security is inherited from its parent. In other words, security roles assigned to the **Home** folder will be inherited by all child folders. If you attempt to set explicit security roles to a child folder, you will receive the message shown in Figure 9.6.

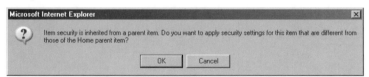

Figure 9.6: Warning Message When Attempting to Break Inheritance.

Item Roles

Item roles are assigned to specific items, such as folders, as opposed to a system role, which affects the management of the server itself. To assign users and groups to item roles, follow these simple steps:

1 Open Report Manager in Internet Explorer.

2 Navigate to the desired folder on which you will set security.

3 Click the **Properties** tab.

4 Click the **Security** sub-tab. You will see a list of groups and users and their roles for security on the selected object. If you are setting security on the **Home** folder, **Security** is the only sub-tab shown.

5 To edit the role assignments, simply click the **Edit** link next to the user or group. To add a new role assignment, click the **New Role Assignment** button. Either way, you will see a screen similar to the one in Figure 9.5. The only difference is that the displayed list of roles will be item-level roles instead of system-level roles.

6 If you are editing an assignment, click the **Apply** button to save your changes or **Cancel** to discard your changes. Click the **New Role** button to assign a new system-level role and bring up the screen shown in Figure 9.3. You can also click the **Delete Role Assignment** button to remove the current role assignment from the system. This will not delete the system role itself, only the assignment to the user or group.

7 If you are adding a new role assignment, click the **OK** button to save your changes or **Cancel** to discard your changes. Click the **New Role** button to assign a new system-level role and bring up the screen shown in Figure 9.3. The security account that you enter will be validated before the role assignment is saved.

Encryption

It is a very good idea to use SSL (Secure Sockets Layer) encryption for any Web-based application, including Report Server and Report Manager, which transmits data over the wire. It is even more important when transmitting data over the Internet or Extranet, or when transmitting sensitive data. Without encryption, data is transmitted in clear text, so anyone with special hardware or software designed to trap, or *sniff,* TCP/IP packets, can see the data. However, if the web pages are accessed using HTTPS (Secure HTTP), an SSL certificate encrypts the data going across the wire.

SSL works by placing a digital file, known as a *certificate* on your web server. Certificates can be obtained by a certified authority, such as Thawte (www.thawte.com) or Verisign (www.verisign.com). The certified authority sends the certificate back to you after they have verified basic company information and charged you a fee. Alternatively, you can generate your own certificate using Windows 2000 or Windows 2003 Server, but users will receive an error that the certificate is not from a trusted source. Once you receive the digital certificate from the trusted source, install it on your web server. You know that your web site is secure when you see the lock icon in the bottom right-hand corner of the Internet Explorer window.

Summary

Security is a very important part of any application, but especially web-based applications. There are several ways to secure your reports using SQL Server Reporting Services. Because SQL Server Reporting Services uses a role-based security model, it is very easy to use existing roles or to assign new roles. In addition to managing roles, you assign predefined tasks to those roles. Once you manage roles and tasks, you can assign users and groups to those roles. Users and groups can be defined on the reporting server itself, or on domain accounts.

Chapter 10

Server
Monitoring

An important aspect of understanding the health of your report server is to monitor the activity and status of the server. As with all SQL Server Reporting Services activities, monitoring your system is very easy to do, but you must know what is available to be monitored on the server. This chapter shows you the basics of monitoring and configuring the report server.

Logs

If configured to do so, your report server will log many activities. It will log events that happen on the report server, reports that are run, and many other aspects of your report server. To configure your server to keep these logs, see the section "System Settings" later in this chapter.

Logs are stored as text files and contain much data. The log files are stored on the same drive as your SQL Server Reporting Services installation, according to the following directory structure:

SYNTAX
```
<<drive>>\Program Files\<<instance>>\MSSQL\Reporting Services\LogFiles
```

EXAMPLE
```
C:\Program Files\Microsoft SQL Server\MSSQL\Reporting Services\LogFiles
```

There are three types of files stored in this folder:

- ▶ **ReportServer** — Logs for the report Web server.

- ▶ **ReportServerService** — Logs for the reporting server.

- ▶ **ReportServerWebApp** — Logs for the report manager.

The reporting server stores the three types of logs with file names that include the type of file, as well as the date/time the file was created. Here is the syntax:

SYNTAX

```
<<filetype>>_<<datestamp>>.log
```

EXAMPLE

```
ReportServer_12_01_2003_09_00_00.log
```

> **FREE** *Bonus:*
>
> Each of these files contains quite a bit of information about your reports, but is too voluminous to list here. To help you view these log files on your own server, a free utility is available that you can download on the web site for this book at **www.rationalpress.com.**

Performance

As with all servers, it is important to understand the health of your report server by monitoring its performance. Monitoring performance allows you to predict when you will have bottlenecks and other problems. Monitoring your server also allows you to spot trends in performance to determine if there are specific reports that are not performing well, or if too many people are running reports at the same time.

Because SQL Server Reporting Services runs on a web server, performance is monitored by using the Windows Performance Monitor. However, when you installed SQL Server Reporting Services, additional performance counters were also installed for specifically monitoring your reporting server. *Performance counters* are components that monitor, or count, one specific performance metric for a server or an application. These performance counters watch for server or application metrics and log its findings in a standard way for you to view.

SQL Server Reporting Services installs approximately fifty (50) performance counters that you can use to monitor the health of your server.

Using Performance Counters

Before you can use performance counters, you must open the Windows Performance Monitor. To use performance counters, follow these steps:

1   On your report server, open the Performance Monitor by clicking the **Start** ⇨ **Settings** ⇨ **Control Panel** ⇨ **Administrative Tools** ⇨ **Performance** menu.

2   Click the **+** icon to add a new counter to the Performance Monitor.

3   From the **Performance object** dropdown list, select either the **Reporting Service** or **Scheduling and Delivery Processes** categories.

4   Select the desired performance counter(s) from the category selected in the previous step. Details about each counter can be found by clicking the **Explain** button or in the SQL Server Reporting Services online help.

5   Click the **Add** button to add the selected counter(s) to the Performance Monitor. Figure 10.1 shows what the Performance Monitor looks like with Reporting Services counters added.

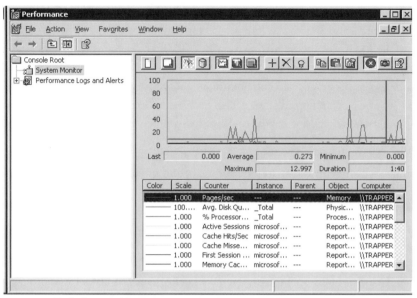

Figure 10.1: The Performance Monitor.

You can run the Performance Monitor for as long as you would like in order to view your server's performance. You can even set alerts for your counters or log them to a file. More details about using the Performance Monitor can be found in the Windows Server online documentation.

System Settings

SQL Server Reporting Services allow anyone assigned to the **System Administrator** role to configure a few settings that affect the performance of your server. SQL Server Reporting Services roles are discussed in Chapter 9.

The areas configurable by the System Administrator include the amount of disk space used on the report server, the report execution timeout, and report logging. All of these configurations are done in the **Site Settings** page. To bring up the **Site Settings** page, click the **Site Settings** link at the top of any page on the reporting server. Figure 10.2 shows this page.

Figure 10.2: The Site Settings Page.

The settings on this page that affect performance are:

▶ **Select the default settings for report history** — This setting affects the retention of the reports. You may choose to allow unlimited caching of reports, which will potentially use all available disk space, or to limit the number of copies of each report. The default selection is to limit the number of report copies to **10**. Caching is discussed further in Chapter 8.

▶ **Report Execution Timeout** — This setting affects the query performance of your reports. A report can take a long time to run, especially if the query that makes up its data set(s) takes a long time to run or if they are poorly written. You have the option to not limit report execution, or to stop processing (or *timeout*) your reports if they do not finish after a specified period of time. The default value is **1300** seconds, or roughly 22 minutes.

▶ **Enable report execution logging** — Enables the report server to log the actions of the reports that are run, including any errors. This is generally a good idea, but it does take some processing power, memory, and disk space. You can optionally remove log entries that are older than a specified number of days. You probably don't want to keep log files indefinitely, so the default settings will ensure that the log files are removed after **60** days. This log is written back to the report server database. To view this information you should set up the Data Transformation Services, or *DTS*, package (included on the Reporting Services installation CD) to move the data from the report server database to a database of your choice. This is necessary so that you do not impact the performance of the report server by blocking the log table.

Subscriptions

Subscriptions to reports can be monitored on two different levels: users and administrators. A user can monitor the subscriptions that he/she has subscribed to, as well as the properties of those subscriptions. Administrators can monitor system-wide subscription settings. Subscriptions are covered in Chapter 12.

Monitoring Running Jobs

When a report or subscription is running, it runs under the context of a *job* because a unit of work is being executed. Anyone can monitor and manage his/ her own jobs for reports that they initiate, but only someone assigned to the **System Administrator** role can manage system jobs. A *system job* is one that is generated automatically, based on a scheduled event.

To manage running jobs, follow these simple steps:

1 Click the **Site Settings** link at the top of the page.

2 Click the **Manage Jobs** link at the bottom of the page.

3 Assuming you are assigned to the **System Administrator** role,

if you wish to show both personal jobs and system jobs, click the **Show System Jobs** button. Otherwise, only personal jobs will be shown. You will be shown a list of the running jobs, as illustrated in Figure 10.3.

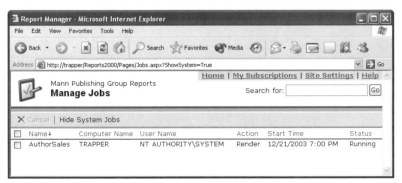

Figure 10.3: Managing Running Jobs.

4   If you wish to terminate any job, click the check box in the left-hand column associated with that job and click the **Cancel** button.

Summary

It is good practice to monitor the health of all of your servers, including your reporting server. Monitoring your server includes activities such as watching its performance over time, its disk space, memory, and more. Additionally, you can control settings related to the performance of your server, such as how logging occurs and when report execution times out. This chapter goes through these options to show how you can be proactive in maintaining your server's health.

Chapter 11

Deploying Reports

Deploying your report project is similar to deploying any kind of web-based project using Visual Studio .NET. The concept behind deployment is that you first create your report project and any desired reports within the project. You also create data sources and data sets, and specify images to be used in your project. Once you have previewed your report using the **Preview** tab in Visual Studio .NET and corrected any errors, you are ready to deploy your report onto a reporting server.

It is recommended that you test your reports in a testing environment before deploying them to your production environment. Although this extra step is not required, it does afford you the opportunity to rigorously test your reporting projects and to make sure that the reports meet the user's needs and conform to their specifications. It also gives users a chance to test the reports without risking undue bandwidth consumption and other production-related nightmares.

Configuration Manager

Visual Studio .NET allows you to specify different configurations of how you will debug and deploy your projects, including Reporting Services projects. Not only is the Configuration Manager effective at helping you configure production settings, it is also used to ensure that when you debug reports running on your workstation, the reporting project is not deployed at the same time. A project should only be deployed when you explicitly indicate that you are ready to deploy your projects.

To use the configuration manager, follow these simple steps:

1   Right-click the name of your solution in the Solution Explorer pane.

2   Select the **Configuration Manager** menu. This brings up the
     Configuration Manager, as shown in Figure 11.1.

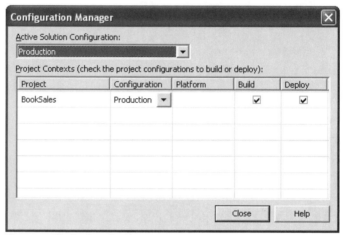

Figure 11.1: The Configuration Manager.

3   Select the desired configuration. By default, your Visual Studio
     .NET environment will contain two installed configurations
     Debug and **Production**. If you are deploying into your production
     environment, select **Production** from the **Active Solution
     Configuration** dropdown list. If you want to create a new
     configuration that isn't in the list, such as a testing configuration,
     click the **<New...>** item from the dropdown list. Creating a new
     item invokes another small dialog box that allows you to name your
     new configuration and optionally copy another configuration into
     the new one as a starting point.

4   In the **Project Contexts** grid below the dropdown list, you will see
     the line items associated with the configuration chosen. You can
     control these aspects of each of your configurations:

- **Project** — If a solution contains more than one project, you must list your projects in the order of dependency in the grid. The order these projects are displayed indicates the dependency order.

- **Platform** — If there is more than one target environment on the computer, you will see a dropdown list of those platforms, such as different versions of the .NET platform. Depending on your system configuration, you may see nothing at all in this list.

- **Build** — Check box that indicates the associated project in the solution will be built (or compiled) when the selected configuration is chosen and the project is deployed.

- **Deploy** — Check box that indicates the associated project in the solution will be deployed to the target server when the selected configuration is chosen and the project is deployed.

5   Make sure to select the desired configuration before clicking the **Close** button. Whatever configuration is chosen when you click the **Close** button will be active in the solution. Only one configuration can be active at any one time.

Deployment Targets

Before you deploy your reporting services project, you must indicate onto which server the project will be deployed. A *deployment target* is simply a URL that includes the IP address or domain name of the target server, as well as the reporting server folder. An example of a deployment target is:

`http://report.mannpublishing.com/ReportServer`

By default, when you deploy your project, Visual Studio .NET will create a folder on the root of the reporting server that is the same name as your project. Then, for each report that you have created, you will see those reports under the new folder. For example, suppose you have a project named **Sales**, which contains three (3) separate reports, named **ByEmployee**, **ByRegion**, and **TotalSales**. When you deploy to a report server target, a **Sales** folder will be automatically created for you and your three reports will exist under that folder.

You must specify one deployment target for each configuration. For more information on configurations, see "Configuration Manager" earlier in this chapter. To specify a deployment target, follow these steps:

1   Right-click the name of your project in the Solution Explorer pane that you wish to deploy.

2   Select the **Properties** menu item. This brings up the properties pane for your selected project, as shown in Figure 11.2.

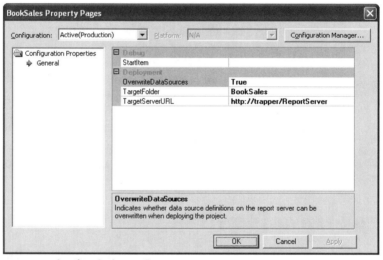

Figure 11.2: Specifying Deployment Targets.

These properties are available for each configuration of a Reporting Services project:

- **OverwriteDataSources** — Indicates whether your data source files (with an RDS extension) will be overwritten on the report server if it exists. By default, this value is **False**.

- **TargetFolder** — The folder in which your reports will be created on the target report server. By default, this value is the same name as the project you are deploying.

- **TargerServerURL** — The URL of the target report server.

3   Click the **OK** button to save your changes and close the dialog box.

Notice the **Configuration** dropdown list in Figure 11.2. It shows the selected configuration of **Production** as being active. When you deploy your solution, it will be deployed using the parameters that you specify on this screen for the currently active configuration. If you wish to change the currently active configuration, you can do so in the Configuration Manager. The concept of the active configuration allows you to configure deployment parameters one time and classify them as a single configuration. Then, when you wish to deploy to a different environment, you simply change the active configuration and deploy your project.

Deploying

Once you have created your desired configurations in the Configuration Manager and configured the deployment target information in the project properties, you're ready to deploy your projects. Deploying couldn't be any easier. Here's how you do it:

1   Right-click the project you wish to deploy in the Solution Explorer pane.

2   Click the **Deploy** menu. If the active configuration specifies that the project will be built, your project is compiled. Then, if you have indicated that the project is to be deployed as part of the active configuration, your project will be deployed.

3   Watch the **Output** window to see if your deployment succeeds or contains errors. Figure 11.3 shows what a failed deployment looks like when you specify an invalid Deployment URL. Fix any errors and redeploy.

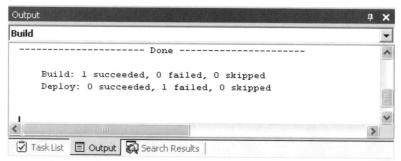

Figure 11.3: Viewing Deployment Errors.

Summary

Deployment is very easy, but not necessarily straight-forward if you've never done it before. If you are a seasoned Visual Studio .NET developer, then this is a piece of cake. You need to understand the concept of configurations and the Configuration Manager. You also need to understand the concept of deployment targets and active configurations. Learning the concepts in this chapter will quickly bring you up to speed in deploying your reporting projects.

Delivering and Using Reports

Chapter 12

Report
Subscriptions

In addition to running on-demand reports, users can also receive reports automatically based on a subscription. A *subscription* allows a report to query a data source, render a report, and deliver the report to a specified target. A subscription report is generated based on triggers that take place on the reporting server, such as a timed event, data changing, or a custom process. A subscription also ensures that users of SQL Server Reporting Services don't have to be sitting at their computers to open a report in the web browser. The report can be delivered to them in an e-mail, or even generated upon a given schedule and placed on a file server.

Subscriptions can only be created for reports that have stored credentials, as in the case of a shared data source or one that is stored with the report. Because a subscription is an automatic function and cannot prompt the user to log in, credentials must be supplied in the data source connection.

There are two types of subscriptions offered by SQL Server Reporting Services:

▶ **Simple** — A report is sent from the server to one or more users or a file share. Simple subscriptions, sometimes known as *push* subscriptions, have predefined parameters and a list of recipients or file share locations.

▶ **Data-driven** — A report that is generated according to dynamic parameters specified with a query and resolved at runtime when the report is rendered. A data-driven subscription does not need predefined recipients, file locations, or parameters. The query retrieves all of these dynamic variables at runtime.

Simple Subscriptions

A simple subscription is defined on the server and indicates which report will be rendered, the recipient(s) or file location to receive the report, and the schedule upon which the report is generated. This type of subscription is called *simple* because the recipients and parameter values are static and it is quite easy to create.

Here's how you create a simple subscription:

1   Create your report using the techniques described in this book.

2   Run your report in a web browser using Report Manager.

3   Click the **Subscriptions** tab or the **New Subscription** button directly.

4   If you clicked the **Subscriptions** tab, you must now click the **New Subscription** button on this screen. Either way, you will see a subscription screen with many options, as shown in Figure 12.1.

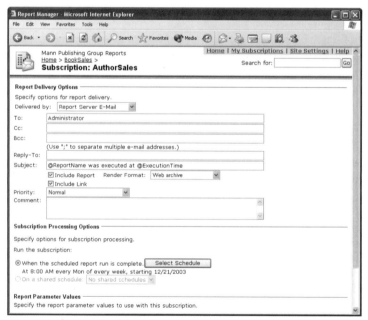

Figure 12.1: Creating a New Subscription.

5   Specify report delivery options. This section allows you to select the delivery options for your report. The option you choose from the **Delivered by** dropdown list dictates which options become available on the screen. If you choose a value of **Report Server E-Mail**, you must specify e-mail related properties, such as **To**, **Cc**, **Bcc**, **Reply-To**, **Subject**, **Priority**, and **Comment**. If you choose a value of **Report Server File Share**, you must specify file-related properties, such as **File Name**, **Path**, **Credentials**, and **Overwrite options**.

Regardless of the option you choose, you must also indicate the **Render Format**. You have a choice of the following:

- **HTML with Office Web Components** (This option is only available for file shares)

- **Excel**

- **Web archive** (This is the default option)

- **Acrobat (PDF) file**

- **TIFF file**

- **CSV (comma delimited)**

- **XML file with report data**

6   Indicate your scheduling choices. You have the following scheduling choices:

- **When the scheduled report run is complete** — This option allows you to specify scheduling parameters when you click the **Select Schedule** button.

- **On a shared schedule** — This option allows you to select a schedule that has already been created for use by multiple reports.

7   Fill-in parameter values. If your report contains parameters, you will be prompted at the bottom of the screen to select or enter values for each of the parameters that should be used when the report is run.

8   Click the **OK** button to save your choices.

Data-Driven Subscriptions

In contrast to a simple subscription, in which you must specify static values at design time, a data-driven subscription allows you to specify a data set to retrieve values at runtime. A data-driven subscription lets you to retrieve the following values from a data set:

▶ **Subscriber list** — A list of recipients for the subscription.

▶ **User-specific delivery preferences** — The type of report delivery (PDF, HTML, etc.) for each individual subscriber.

▶ **Parameters** — The parameters expected by a report.

One major advantage to using a data-driven subscription is that you can have hundreds or thousands of e-mail addresses as recipients. It would be virtually impossible to enter all these e-mail address manually. Data-driven subscriptions make large recipient lists very manageable.

Creating a data-driven subscription is done in seven distinct steps, following a web-based wizard. Here's how to start the wizard:

1   Run your desired report.

2   Click the **Subscriptions** tab.

3   Click the **New Data-driven Subscription** button. The wizard starts.

Then, walk through each of the seven steps in the wizard:

1   Enter basic data about the subscription, such as the description, delivery method, and data source. Click the **Next** button.

2   Select specific information about the data source. If you indicated that you want to use a shared data source in step 1, you must select the shared data source here. If you indicated a new data source in step 1, you indicate the security credentials for the new data source in this step. Click the **Next** button to continue.

3   Enter the data-driven query that will be used in the report. The data-driven query is a special query that will retrieve results from the database and use them to specify report options. Listing 12.1 shows an example of a data-driven query designed to retrieve contact information.

```
SELECT ac.eMailAddress

FROM   AuthorContact ac

       JOIN AuthorRoyalty ar

       ON ar.AuthorID = ac.AuthorID

WHERE  ar.SentFlag IS NULL
```

Listing 12.1: Sample Data-Driven Query.

The above query will retrieve all e-mail addresses for authors with royalty statements that have not already been sent. This effectively allows you to send the report to a different list of recipients each time the report runs without needing to change the query or the report. Click the **Next** button.

4   Map the fields returned from the query in the prior step to the fields that the subscription engine requires to render and deliver a report. Figure 12.2 shows this step, with the **EMailAddress** field returned from the data-driven query being mapped to the **To** field for an e-mail-based subscription. Click **Next** to continue.

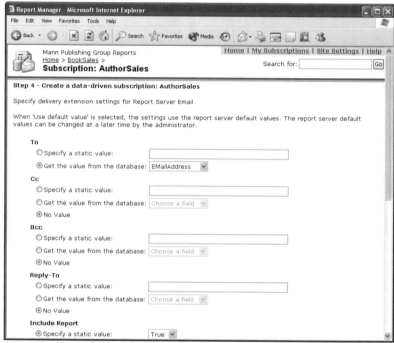

Figure 12.2: Mapping Fields in a Data-Driven Query.

5   Specify a value for each report parameter expected by the report. Click the **Specify a static value** option if you want to enter or select a value that doesn't change for each recipient of the report at runtime. (This is similar to the way you specified parameter values when you created simple subscriptions.) Otherwise, click the **Get the value from the database** option to indicate which field from your data-driven query should be used to supply a value for the parameter. Click **Next** to continue.

6   Indicate how the report is to be processed. You have these options:

●   **When the report data is updated on the report server** — Automatically runs the report when the snapshot is updated. This option is available for simple subscriptions if a snapshot is defined for the report. Click the **Finish** button.

- **On a schedule created for this subscription** — Specifies a schedule for use with this one subscription only. If you click this option, you will specify a schedule in the next step. Click the **Next** button when you are ready to continue.

- **On a shared schedule** — Selects a previously defined shared schedule from the dropdown list. Click the **Finish** button.

7   If you selected the **On a schedule created for this subscription** option in the previous step, you must now specify scheduling options for the subscription. Click the **Finish** button.

Managing Subscriptions

Viewing, editing, and deleting subscriptions are all handled in the **My Subscriptions** web page or on the **Subscription** tab for a specific report. To manage subscriptions, the user follows these simple steps:

1   Click the **My Subscriptions** link at the top of any web page or the **Subscription** tab of any report.

2   To edit a subscription, click the **Edit** link associated with the desired subscription. You will see a page that is identical to the one you used to create your subscription, as described in the section, "Simple Subscriptions," earlier in this chapter.

3   To delete a subscription, click the check box in the left-hand column and click the **Delete** button.

Summary

Subscriptions are a very productive way for the server to send reports in a desired format to one or more recipients or file locations. You can configure two types of subscriptions: simple or data-driven. In simple subscriptions, all parameters are static and are specified when you create the subscription. In data-driven subscriptions, parameters are specified in the results of a query and they can vary at runtime. Furthermore, data-driven subscriptions can run when the data that makes up the query changes in the underlying database.

Chapter 13

Internet
Explorer

Because SQL Server Reporting Services runs on Internet Information Services (IIS) as a Web Service, you won't be surprised to learn that Internet Explorer is a core part of using this technology. Internet Explorer version 6.0 is required for most administrative functions.

Internet Explorer can be used to perform these functions within SQL Server Reporting Services:

> ► Run on-demand (pull) reports (covered in this chapter)

> ► Manage shared data sources (see Chapter 4)

> ► Upload files to a folder (see Chapter 8)

> ► Manage security (see Chapter 9)

> ► Manage configuration parameters (see Chapter 10)

> ► Create simple and data-driven subscriptions (see Chapter 12)

Running On-Demand Reports

An *on-demand* report is sometimes called a *pull* report because the user requests a report and specifies parameters at will from a browser. An on-demand report is pulled from the server to the workstation. An on-demand report can be run by specifying a URL in one of three ways:

1   Navigating within the **Reports** virtual root folder, which is used by the Report Manager application.

2   Navigating within the **ReportServer** virtual root folder, which is used for accessing the server as a Web Service.

3   Specifying the report and parameters in the URL.

Using the Reports Virtual Folder

The reports virtual folder was specified when you installed SQL Server Reporting Services. By default, the name of the reports virtual folder is simply **Reports**. Therefore, here is the URL syntax:

SYNTAX

```
http://<<Server>>/<<Reports_Dir>>
```

EXAMPLE

```
http://www.mannpublishing.com/Reports
```

The reports virtual folder is a nicely designed web page that allows you to control most aspects of your reporting server (depending on security privileges) and also to run the reports. Figure 13.1 shows the **Reports** virtual folder.

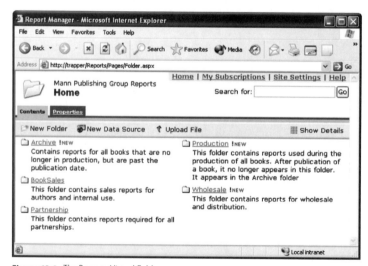

Figure 13.1: The Reports Virtual Folder.

To view the contents of a folder, simply click the link next to the folder icon. To change the properties of the currently displayed folder, click the **Properties** tab. If you have security privileges to do so, you can change security and description of a folder under the **Properties** tab.

If you click a folder that contains reports, you can run any of those reports by clicking the associated link. An example of running a report named **AuthorSales** is shown in Figure 13.2. Notice that you must select values for one parameter defined for the report. The parameter, named **Year**, is a dropdown list of values. Once you select values for the required parameters in any report, click the **View Report** button to render the report. Otherwise, if there are no required parameters, the report will run immediately.

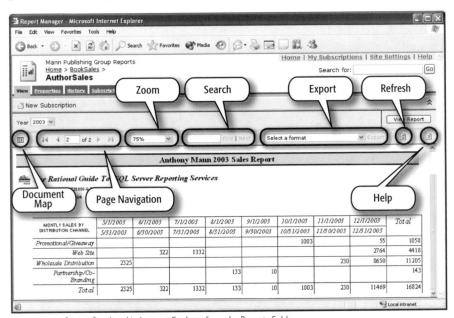

Figure 13.2: Report Rendered in Internet Explorer from the Reports Folder.

You can navigate through the web-based interface in Internet Explorer. Figure 13.2 outlines the specific areas of the screen that help you navigate and render your reports.

Using the Report Server Virtual Folder

The Report Server virtual folder allows you to access your reports, but does not provide the same interface as the **Reports** virtual folder. You cannot see description information, or change anything. It does, however, allow you to navigate through the folder structure to find reports and the resources used on those reports, such as pictures and data sources. By default, the name of the report server virtual folder is simply **ReportServer**. Here is the URL syntax:

SYNTAX

```
http://<<Server>>/<<Report_Server_Dir>>
```

EXAMPLE

```
http://www.mannpublishing.com/ReportServer
```

Figure 13.3 shows the **ReportServer** virtual folder.

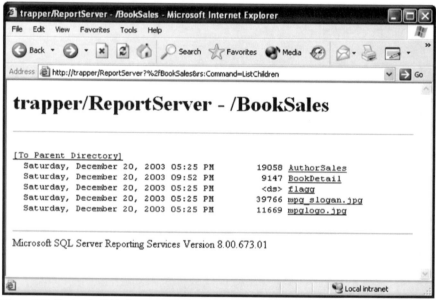

Figure 13.3: Viewing the Folder Structure of the ReportServer Virtual Folder.

You can run a report simply by clicking the name of the report, as you do when navigating the **Reports** virtual folder.

Specifying URL Parameters

Instead of navigating through the folder structure of your report server, you can run a report directly by specifying the exact parameters needed by the server in the URL of Internet Explorer.

This is the syntax for using the URL to access a report:

SYNTAX

```
<<protocol>>://<<server>>/<<report_server>>?[/<<path>>]
&<<prefix:>><<param>>=<<value>>[&<<prefix>>:<<param>>=<<value>>]...n]
```

Variables:

- ▶ <<protocol>> is either HTTP or HTTPS (for SSL encryption).

- ▶ <<server>> is the name of your reporting server.

- ▶ <<report_server>> is the name of your virtual folder for the report server.

- ▶ <<path>> is the full path of the report RDL file, without the RDL file extension.

- ▶ <<prefix>> is the name of the prefix that accesses a specific report server process, such as **rc**, **rs**, **dsu**, **dsp**. See the Reporting Services online documentation for more information about using these prefixes.

- ▶ <<param>> is the name of your parameter, such as **Year**.

- ▶ <<value>> is the actual value to assign to the parameter, such as **2003**.

EXAMPLE

```
http://www.mannpublishing.com/ReportServer2000?/BookSales/
AuthorSales&Year=2003
```

The example shown above will run the same report as the one in Figure 13.2, but this report has all of its parameters specified in the URL. The advantage of running reports from the URL command-line is that user interaction is not required. As long as you supply the required parameter values, the report can run.

You might want to consider using SSL to secure your report server. This is because you might be passing sensitive information needed to gain access to a specific record, as in the case of a social security number. If you secure the web site with 128-bit SSL, the parameters and data are encrypted when they are sent across the Internet. See Chapter 9 for more information about SSL.

Summary

Most report activity, except for creating reports themselves, can be done by using Internet Explorer. However, there are third-party tools on the market that allow report creation over the web. Internet Explorer can render reports in a variety of formats. It can even bypass user intervention by specifying parameters on the URL command-line. In any event, you should consider securing your reporting server with SSL for use with Internet Explorer and all other means of accessing SQL Server Reporting Services.

Chapter 14

SharePoint Technologies

SQL Server Reporting Services allows reports to be integrated with many different technologies. Not surprisingly, one of those technologies is Microsoft SharePoint. There are two "flavors" of SharePoint technologies:

▶ **Windows SharePoint Services** — Built into Windows Server 2003, this technology allows you to create team-oriented sites for sharing resources and collaborate with other users on the team.

▶ **SharePoint Portal Server 2003** — This separately licensed product provides many of the features of Windows SharePoint Services. It embraces the concept of a portal to serve as a digital dashboard, and expands upon the "team" concept to allow additional capabilities such as personalized sites and single sign-on.

SharePoint technologies work by displaying pieces of information in a specific area of the screen. These pieces are known as web parts. There are many standard web parts available from Microsoft, or you can develop your own for specific custom functionality. The Microsoft web parts are either available in an online gallery or automatically installed with the products into a local gallery of web parts. More information about Microsoft SharePoint technologies and costs can be found on the web at www.microsoft.com/sharepoint.

Tech Tip:

If you install SQL Server Reporting Services on the same physical machine as any SharePoint technology, you will have some difficulties activating the reporting server. There are a couple of specific steps you need to follow, which are outlined in the README file on the SQL Server Reporting Services CD.

SharePoint Portal Server 2003

It is quite easy to integrate SQL Server Reporting Services with SharePoint Portal Server 2003. SharePoint Portal Server 2003 (and version 2001) allows you to specify a file share or a URL using built-in web parts. Therefore, you can easily include any aspect of SQL Server Reporting Services in your portal. To prepare for further discussion, refer to Figure 14.1, which includes a standard **Page Viewer Web Part** that displays the **My Subscriptions** page for SQL Server Reporting Services.

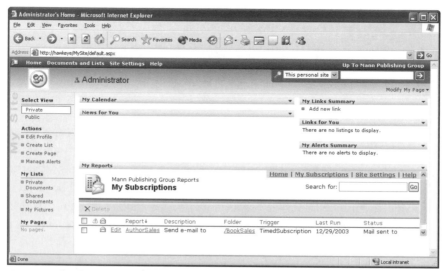

Figure 14.1: SharePoint Portal Server 2003 Showing the Page Viewer Web Part.

Even if you are not familiar with SharePoint Portal Server 2003, you can see in Figure 14.1 that the **My Reports** area contains the **My Subscriptions** page from SQL Server Reporting Services in Report Manager. It is quite simple to implement this functionality by following these steps:

1   Within SharePoint Portal Server 2003, navigate to the **My Site** page.

2   Click the **Modify My Page** ⇨ **Add Web Parts** ⇨ **Browse** menu. This brings up a small **Add Web Parts** window to allow you to browse through the available web parts.

3   Browse to the web part called **Page Viewer Web Part**.

4   Drag and drop the web part to the desired area of the screen.

5   Close the **Add Web Parts** window.

6   You'll notice a phrase in the newly placed web part area that reads:

> To link to content, open the tool pane and then type a URL in the Link text box.

> Click the **open the tool pane** link, which brings up the **Page Viewer** window, as shown in Figure 14.2.

Figure 14.2: Customizing the Page Viewer Web Part.

7   Enter the URL of the **My Subscriptions** page, following this
     syntax:

SYNTAX

```
http://<<Server>>/<<Reports_Dir>>/Pages/Subscriptions.aspx
```

EXAMPLE

```
http://trapper/Reports/Pages/Subscriptions.aspx
```

8   Click the **OK** button.

Alternatively, you can use the same concepts to ensure that SQL Server Reporting
Services delivers reports to a file share upon a specific subscription schedule.
Then, you can use the same **Page Viewer Web Part** to show the contents of that
folder instead of a web page. An example of a folder containing two reports is
shown in Figure 14.3.

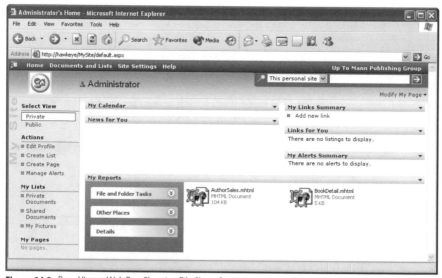

Figure 14.3: Page Viewer Web Part Showing File Share Contents.

Windows SharePoint Services

Windows SharePoint Services allows you to create a team-oriented site on
Windows Server 2003. This service is not installed as part of the server installation,

so you must install it separately. For more information about SharePoint Services, visit the Microsoft web site at http://www.microsoft.com/windowsserver2003.

You manage web parts in Windows SharePoint Services just as you do for SharePoint Portal Server 2003. Figure 14.4 shows a sample Windows SharePoint Services site with the same **My Subscription** URL in the **Page Viewer Web Part** shown in Figure 14.1.

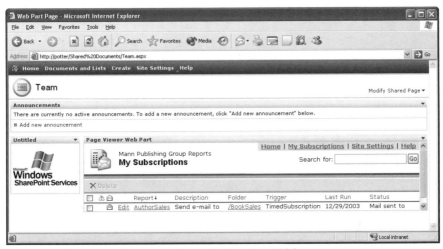

Figure 14.4: Windows SharePoint Services Showing the Page Viewer Web Part.

Summary

Integration of SQL Server Reporting Services with SharePoint technologies can be quite simple. These technologies include a generic web part that allows the display and rendering of web pages. You can also use the same web part to show folder contents with just a simple configuration change.

You can also develop custom web parts in Visual Studio .NET. These custom web parts can access the SQL Server Reporting Services Web Service to achieve any desired functionality, but doing so is not shown in this book. Look for an upcoming book by Rational Press at www.rationalpress.com on building SharePoint web parts.

Chapter 15

Microsoft Office

Microsoft Office is another application that SQL Server Reporting Services integrates with right out of the box. A common need in reporting solutions is to manipulate report data in a spreadsheet program, like Microsoft Excel. With SQL Server Reporting Services, this couldn't be any easier.

Integration with Microsoft Office requires that your workstation have Office XP or later installed, or Office Web Components. This chapter shows you the basics of the integration points between SQL Server Reporting Services and Microsoft Office.

Excel

Excel is the most common Microsoft Office application to integrate with SQL Server Reporting Services. This is because reporting solutions lend themselves to spreadsheet-type applications to allow manipulation of data. After all, you display report data in a table or matrix, so exporting to Excel is a logical extension to these formats.

Exporting a report to Excel is extremely simple. To export a report, follow this procedure:

1   Run a report in Internet Explorer.

2   In the export dropdown list in the Report Viewer toolbar, click the **Excel** option.

3   Click the **Export** button.

4   You will have the choice to open or save the newly created Excel workbook.

The first worksheet in the Excel workbook will be a document map, if the report is configured to use document maps. Every other worksheet in the workbook will be the individual pages, or sections, of the original report. For example, look at the report in Figure 15.1 which is rendered as an Excel workbook.

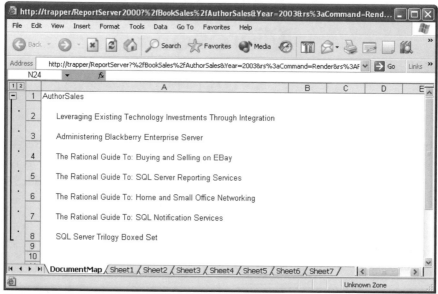

Figure 15.1: Report Exported to an Excel Workbook, showing the Document Map.

Figure 15.1 shows an Excel workbook with eight worksheets. The first is a document map to help navigate through the other worksheets. The other seven worksheets represent the different pages of the report. The document map provides the same functionality as it does in the report. To navigate to a specific page in the report, simply click the item in the document map or click the sheet name at the bottom of screen. Figure 15.2 shows **Sheet 4** of the report worksheet, after clicking an item in the document map. Notice how it looks very similar to the way reports are rendered in HTML.

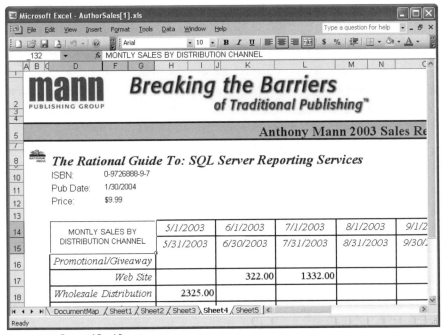

Figure 15.2: Exported Excel Report.

There are some rules that you must keep in mind before exporting data to Excel. Some of the limitations are:

▶ Excel can only display up to 65,536 rows of data per worksheet.

▶ Excel can only display up to 256 columns of data per worksheet.

▶ A single cell in a worksheet can only contain 32,767 characters.

All of the limitations and considerations of exporting reports to Excel are discussed in the SQL Server Reporting Services online help. It shows some advanced concepts, like changing device information settings, which are XML configurations for export rendering to specific devices or environments.

Office Web Components

If you are going to use Office functionality in your web pages, such as charts, graphs, Excel worksheets, and pivot tables, you must have either Office or Office Web Components (OWC) installed on your workstation. OWC, version 10 or later is required. These are the same components that are available in Office XP or later. More information on Office Web Components is available by searching for "Office Web Components" on the Microsoft Office web site at http://office.microsoft.com.

Exporting to the OWC format will create an HTML page that contains built-in interactive functionality. Interactivity is achieved through the OWC components (which are ActiveX components) communicating with the report server from a web page.

To use OWC, export your report in the **HTML with Office Web Components** format, exactly the same way you export to any other format. The **HTML with Office Web Components** format is especially useful when you wish to provide pivot table functionality in your reports. Exporting to the **Excel** format creates each section on a separate worksheet within the workbook. On the other hand, OWC includes an ActiveX Excel component in the Report Manager web page that provides pivot table functionality. Figure 15.3 shows a pivot table from the sample **Company Sales** report after you export to the **HTML with Office Web Components** format.

Notice in Figure 15.3 that the ActiveX component actually provides a subset of the Excel toolbars. You can also right-click any heading or cell to invoke additional context-sensitive options. Exporting to the **HTML with Office Web Components** format is the only way to achieve out of the box pivot table functionality.

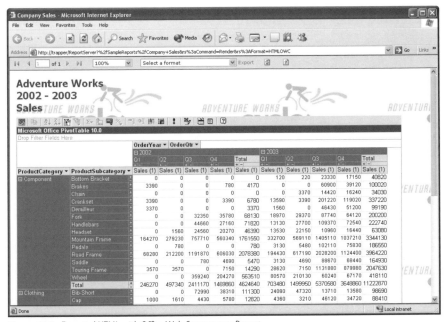

Figure 15.3: Exported HTML with Office Web Components Report.

Summary

SQL Server Reporting Services makes it very easy to view reports using Microsoft Office technologies, like Excel. You can export a report directly into an Excel workbook (using version XP or later), or use Office Web Components in an HTML page to achieve true pivot table functionality. Your options are completely open.